Parenting the Sensitive Child

Guidelines and practices

Parenting the Sensitive Child
Guidelines and practices

Editor: Jean Jacoby

Cover design: Brett Armstrong Advertising

Layout and typeset: John Bertram, Tangerine Design

Printed by AYM Printers

Queries may be addressed to pluke@polka.co.za

ISBN 1-4392-0032-7

Contents

Acknowledgements

First and foremost, I want to acknowledge my family. To my wife, Linda, and to my children Dylan, Megan and Matthew; because of you I have been able to write this book from the heart. Thank you for all that you mean to me.

Many of the ideas presented in this book have emerged from nights and days spent in conversation and writing with my dear friend and colleague; Rod Charlton. Rod is a born coach. I am always challenged by his perspectives, and inspired by his energy and attitude towards life. Thank you for your encouragement my friend.

Thank you to Jean Jacoby for her patience and excellent insights as my editor. Thank you too, to Julia Denny-Dimitriou, who has so generously given of her time and wonderful expertise towards the latter end of this project. I know that the guidance that I received from both these people enriched the book enormously.

Of course, this book could never have been written if it weren't for the parents who have allowed me to share some of their journey with them. Thank you to all of you for your trust and your many demonstrations of parental courage. I hope you know how much I have learned from each one of you.

Rob Pluke

Foreword

In the following pages you will be called into a world of what the Jesuit John Haughey calls *equipoise*. He prefers this term to *balance*, which sounds static and passive. Equipoise is a state of dynamic balance, which is always under review. A tightrope walker does not balance — rather, she constantly corrects imbalances. As parents, equipoise is a place of creative tension between the many conflicts provoked within us by our children's encounters with an often cruel world. It is in this context that Rob gives us a bold invitation: to manage ourselves purposefully and resist reacting against our sensitive children. Parenting exposes us all, but Rob proposes a place of vulnerability where we can meet our children as unique creatures separate from ourselves. As you will see, he does this with the concern, firmness, gentleness, and acceptance that have become characteristic of his daily practise with children. While these attributes are also very evident in his dealings with parents, they are complemented by an expectation that we as adults 'do the right thing'. He goes on to suggest a range of right things — or rather right ways of thinking about and relating to sensitive children. Above all, you will be asked to share a reverence for your children that goes beyond technique. Rob's approach is first and foremost embedded in relationships. And these relationships are, in turn, grounded in the 'craziness', as he puts it, of everyday life. It is in this craziness that many of us parents will finally find ourselves. It is our children's gift to us.

Tim Barry
Clinical Psychologist

Introduction

Aren't our children fantastic! And yet, if you're anything like me, being a parent has brought new dimensions of vulnerability into your life. What happens to our children affects us so much. It's as though each child carries a piece of our hearts, and to watch them totter towards life's rough hands is sometimes more than we can bear.

These vulnerable feelings can really rise when you realise that you have been blessed with a sensitive child. You may start to recognise early on that there's something different about your child. Once you get over your surprise, you may start to anticipate the many situations and challenges that are going to throw your child into an emotional spin. You start to worry! How, you ask yourself, will my child survive out there?

In this book I want to offer you a cluster of approaches that you can take to the challenge of parenting a sensitive child. As I've had the privilege of working with a wide range of families I've come to appreciate that raising a sensitive child can be a confusing and, at times, gut-wrenching experience. Many of us are typically finely-tuned to our children's emotions. When they are content, we feel at ease. Life is good! However, when our children aren't settled our own stress levels tend to rocket. As we search for ways to soothe our children we may find ourselves feeling uncertain, perhaps at odds with our partners and frustrated by the simplistic advice of well-meaning onlookers.

I believe that the ideas that follow can help you to nurture confidence and resilience in your child. I hope that this new information will give you a clearer sense of direction; that you will know what to aim for when your child is having difficulties, which will help you to feel more confident in your moment-by-moment choices.

At the same time, I need to say that working with sensitive children has been a humbling experience for me. Emotional growth can take an awfully long time. Almost all parents of older sensitive children tell me that their children continue to go through good and bad patches. This is perhaps a bit disheartening, but I think it's realistic. Let me say at the outset, then, that this book is about *growing* rather than *changing* your sensitive child.

Guidelines as opposed to treatment

As the title of this book suggests, I aim to give parents of sensitive children accessible guidelines to use in the normal craziness of family life. Although many of these suggestions might apply to children who are battling with actual clinical difficulties, such as panic attacks, phobias, or depression, this book is not a treatment manual. It offers approaches and perspectives that I believe can prompt sensitive children towards healthy, happy and productive lives. Again, the emphasis is on *growth* rather than *treatment*.

Also, over and above *technique*, this book is about *attitude*. When it comes to raising emotionally sensitive children, I believe that even if you know all the techniques in the world, you'll still flounder if your attitude isn't right. Techniques have to be based in our attitudes. We have to spend some time reflecting on what it is that we're aiming for in the first place. So, with a combination of attitude and technique, I will be delighted if, at the end of this book, you are left with a clearer sense of purpose and direction as a parent.

Be selective

Parenting takes us into unpredictable terrain and we need to remain nimble-footed as we seek to be a positive influence on our children's lives. Not all of the ideas in this book will apply to your child. Some of them are appropriate only at particular stages of a child's life, so pick and choose your way through them. And, please don't underestimate your own parental wisdom: no one knows your child better than you do.

Chapter 1

What do I mean by the label 'sensitive child'?

Sensitive children are easily jangled by daily events.

Some time ago I heard a talk by the internationally-acclaimed family therapist, the late Gianfranco Cecchin. He took care to describe his opinions as 'useful' rather than 'true', and he encouraged a similar humility in his audience. Labels, especially the more psychologically ponderous, invariably involve some force as they slice out their demarcations. Labels place people into categories that often oversimplify and sometimes diminish who they are.

With this in mind, let me say that I'd like this term, the 'sensitive' child', to be used in a flexible, speculative way. Applied well, I trust that it will enrich your understanding of your child's personal experiences. However, see it as useful rather than defining. It's probably fair to say that all children are sensitive in different ways and at different times. So whilst I gather a cluster of children under the banner of 'sensitive', I hope I have done so with a suitably loose embrace.

It's my experience that's left me willing to identify what I describe as 'sensitive children'. Over the years, I have become increasingly interested in the ways that children experience their emotions. I have found that there are youngsters who stand out because they seem to have strong emotional reactions to their environment. It's as though they are somehow *thin skinned*, as though their inner peace is easily jangled by daily events. For them, life is seldom a straight-forward affair. Consequently, many sensitive children come across as timid, anxious and perhaps withdrawn. Because they often seem to run on high-octane fuel, sensitive children can also be quite prickly, vocal, and downright demanding at times. In fact, over the years I've become convinced that many children who present with behaviour problems are sensitive at heart. When challenged, these children come at the world with their fists raised, even though they may feel quite lost on the inside.

Here are three examples:

Michael's ability to bellow was a prominent feature for the maternity ward nurses. Now that he's edged his way into Grade 1, he takes ages to get dressed in the morning and can throw some impressive tantrums on the way to school. He settles down quite well once he's in the classroom, but his teacher has noticed that he hangs back from his peers and he's reluctant to get involved in games during break-time. Michael's just about over his fear of the dark but he still worries a lot about 'baddies'.

Stephanie delights her teachers and intimidates the boys. Her work is exquisitely presented, she participates in a range of sports and she is captain of the school's debating team. Stephanie has good friends, although they're quite a competitive bunch. Last year she was really rattled when one of her friends was awarded academic colours while she wasn't, and her family dreads a negative outcome when next year's prefects are named. Stephanie gets really tired and down sometimes but she just gets angry when her parents suggest that she pushes herself too hard.

All of David's friends agree that he is one of the most relaxed guys on the block. Undeniably talented, he appears irritatingly content with the middle road. Last year he was invited to try for the 1st Rugby XV but he refused, saying he'd prefer to play on the same team as his friends. David often complains of feeling bored. When he brags about his latest play station scores, his father doesn't know whether to 'high five' or shake him.

For me, the lights start to flash when I notice that a child feels distressed when faced with everyday, age-appropriate demands. I also take note of the intensity of distress and whether these strong feelings negatively affect the habitual choices that a child makes. Is he battling to cope in important areas of his life? Is he starting to avoid some of life's opportunities because of an underlying inclination to 'play it safe'? Is her overall sense of happiness or satisfaction somehow limited because of her emotional fragility?

The checklist that follows highlights some of the common features of a 'sensitive child'. You might like to tick those features that you recognise in your own child, or that concern you the most, and keep them in mind as you read further.

As an infant and toddler
dislikes loud noises
takes time to settle in unfamiliar situations or with unfamiliar people
reacts with strong emotions: cries easily
difficult to settle, once upset
may be physically tense
distressed by changes in routine

As a child
seems to lack confidence
may be less independent than other children
prefers a few, select friends
dislikes staying away from home
may try to avoid school, particularly during transitions
can be quite rigid about social rules
tends to be a perfectionist or to worry about faults
worries about a wide range of things (e.g. the dark, not being fetched from school, getting into trouble)
may be physically awkward or tense
complains of tummy aches or headaches during times of stress
is sensitive to discipline
finds certain movies, programmes or stories upsetting
Is affected by other children's distress
is often surprisingly insightful/wise
tends to play it safe

As a teen
can be emotionally closed or fragile
has 'big' emotions
tends to keep friends at arms length
sometimes avoids challenges/stops short of her potential
can become pessimistic or moody
worries about a wide range of things (e.g. looks, relationships, sporting or academic performance)
works too hard, or avoids school demands
tends to be a perfectionist who is not easily satisfied
may be physically insecure

	shows artistic ability
	is easily upset or hurt
	often copes by withdrawing
	struggles to handle competition appropriately
	has a very keen sense of right and wrong
	is very compassionate (good with children or animals)
	asks profound questions

....

As you can see from the above list, I'm asking you to explore a very tender part of your child's experience. This is territory of the heart, so we need to be gentle with our new insights and choices. None of these regions can be taken by force. As parents, we have to be brave enough to enter. Our children need our help. But we should pick our way forward with care, and we should probably take our shoes off at the gate.

Chapter 2

Know the Core but see the Variety

Our children are always more than
the ways they are known

A young mother woke up in the small hours of the night to find her scientist husband sitting at the end of the bed, head in hands. As a new parent her first instinct was to listen out for their infant's now-familiar cry. Silence. With rising concern she asked him what was wrong, what could possibly be more important than a few extra hours of precious sleep? Rousing himself from his deep contemplation, he replied that he was just trying to figure out some method to bring order and peace to their parenting nightmare. Being a sensible woman, she allowed herself a half smile before flopping down and going back to sleep.

We like to understand our world, to make it predictable and apparently more controllable. We divide things up into recognisable categories (such as cause/consequence; normal/abnormal; success/failure). Of course we do the same thing with people, not least our children. Very early on, we start drawing conclusions about who our children are and, importantly, what we can expect from them. And, of course, our children are inclined to act in ways that confirm and cement our expectations. We establish lasting patterns of parent-child interaction.

This is normal, but it isn't always beneficial. It depends on what we assume we know about our children. Sometimes, the things we think we know about them limits who they can be.

We have to remind ourselves that when it comes to our children, there's a critical difference between *knowing* and *seeing*. Both are necessary. I want children to sense that their parents know their core; that they are recognised and profoundly cherished as essentially lovely and good. This secure foundation, embedded in their hearts, enables children to build expansive lives.

However, like all people, children are always more than the ways that they are known. Yes, we have been with our children from the year dot, but this doesn't mean that we know what they can be. We don't know, and ultimately can't control, what our children are going to make of their lives. As a parent, I'm so relieved. There's no way that I'd want to take on that kind of responsibility for my children. The ongoing, exciting process of living, of becoming, belongs to each one of them. Right now, your child is actively creating who he is becoming. He is brimming with a variety of ways of being. He is a kaleidoscope of possibilities. All kinds of advantages emerge when you are able to see that, to recognise it's unfolding.

When it comes to our children, we need to *know the core, but see the variety*. Unfortunately, I think that we often get this mixed up, especially if we are going through a bad patch with our children. In these times, we are inclined to *see the core and know the varieties*. Or, in other words, there's nothing new in the air. Our children's bad actions lead us to think (and often say) that there's something wrong with them *at the core*, which carries the heavy implication that all resulting varieties are likely to be similarly tainted. Our 'bad behaviour' radars are sensitised and we keep seeing more evidence of the faulty core (*"Why are you so...?"*). Unconsciously, we start to expect more of the same. It's very difficult for a child to escape this unintended snare.

If you have a sensitive child, it's quite possible that you are beginning to form some negative or perhaps even despairing assumptions. The world does not always make time and space for sensitive children. They rarely come out of the starting blocks running. In fact they can be frustratingly cautious and slow to put their abilities to work. It's so easy for us to get frustrated, and to start to doubt who our children are and, consequently, who they can be.

For instance, many sensitive children are often called 'shy', a label that can end up being as limiting as it is descriptive. We have to be careful of what we are assuming when we use the word *shy*. While we might know that many sensitive children are initially unsettled by new people and places (Kagan, 2004) it's not accurate to say that sensitive people don't have a sense of humour, or can't be talkative and fun. It's our job to see that! 'Shy' people are very varied. No two are the same. Many people who have been called shy tell me that this label has become like a social prison, preventing them from interacting in authentic ways with the people who claim to 'know' them in this potentially limiting way. People who have carried this label into adulthood invariably tell me that they aren't always quiet and reserved; that they act differently with different people, often according to the expectations that go with each context.

I was amazed when a fellow parent approached me at school to say how much he'd enjoyed a speech my son gave. Apparently he was confident, articulate and really funny. My son? The same guy who won't use the telephone? The same guy who often only mumbles back when adults ask him a question? The same guy whom I keep worrying about? I can only shake my head.

So I encourage you deliberately to see the variety in your child. Make an effort to see him anew each day. I appreciate that it can be really tough to take this stance when your child seems to keep making the same mistakes. But I believe that being lovingly curious about your growing child keeps your relationship dynamic and fertile. 'Seeing' your child helps you to join your child on the exciting borders of his current experiences. Allow your child many opportunities to introduce himself to you. Keep seeing his possibilities!

"The self as an accumulation of experience is a prison; the self as shimmering potentiality, is a prism that, depending on its turning, gives forth many different colours."

– Rosenbaum & Dyckman –

This attitude also encourages more awareness of the variety that is present in every moment of our own lives. So much of life is scripted for us. We are all at risk of living out a role. Making the effort to see the variety in our children slows time down enough for us to be creative rather than just busy. We cannot notice our children effectively when we are stressed. Noticing variety provides instances where we can be caught up in the fun and love of being a family. It's a time when your child can experience you as wholeheartedly present in his world.

Seeing the possibilities in our children requires a combination of time, attitude and words. We have to spend time with them to have any chance of appreciating their diversity. But it can't be parallel time, where we're in the same house but essentially disengaged from each other. We need to clear our minds of clutter, commit ourselves to the moment and really look at our child. And we need to be prepared to describe what we see, so that our children can nourish themselves on our loving observations.

Author and emotional intelligence expert, Daniel Goleman (2006), speaks about how important it is to be able to set aside our own agendas if we want to relate to others with any depth and richness. I'm not sure about you, but I find that I'm far more willing to do this at work than at home. Maybe familiarity makes me careless, but I don't listen to my children with anything like the focus that I offer at work. Truth be told, I'm often more interested in getting them through the evening routines than I am in actually spending time with them. And I know that there are many times when the noise of my selfish ambitions completely obscures the fact that my beloved family is about as precious as precious can get. Embarrassingly, it's even worse when the TV set is on. And if sport is showing, I'm a complete write-off! My body might be in the room, but my mind is a million miles away. My eyes simply don't see what is right in front of me.

I don't want to live like that. But I know that I'll need to be deliberate if I'm going to be able to turn away from the world's babble on anything like a regular basis.

Try this!

- Look up from these pages and see someone from your family. All you have is the present moment. Say something (pleasant) right now that will surprise both of you. You don't even have to discuss it that much.

- Set aside some time to be with your child this week. Don't use the time to solve problems, or to offer advice. Just share yourselves with each other. What would it take to make this a lasting habit?

Renowned author and therapist Paul Pearsall (as quoted in Simon, R. 1999), argues that many of us suffer from *delight deficiency syndrome*. He cautions that "If you don't find a balance between pressure and pleasure, your epitaph is going to read 'Got everything done, died anyway.' (pg 39)" Remind yourself of the possibilities in your world. Don't box the moment in the same old way. And, if needs be, drop the burden of trying to 'improve' your child and simply notice him for a while.

"Life is short. So...? "
— Steven Covey, 'Legacy', The 8th habit —

Chapter 3

Growth versus Change

Growth starts from where your child is, while change makes us dwell on how we'd prefer things to be

Many parents spend hours agonising over the possible causes of their child's emotional difficulties: "Do we expect too much from our child?", "Am I too hard, too soft or too critical?", "Am I over-involved, or am I not involved enough?", "Do we pay too much attention to her sister?" As the list of reasons grows, parents often begin to feel a nagging sense of frustration and powerlessness. Also, many parents have been given *onlooker advice* by family and friends, advice that seems to imply that, somehow, if they were better parents, their children would be more emotionally robust. It's just so easy to blame the parents when a child is battling, but when it comes to a child's emotions, things are seldom that simple.

Of course parents must be thoughtful about their actions, but if you think that something or someone *made* your child this way, you're going to spend your whole life trying to fix her. The thing is; studies show that many emotionally sensitive children are born that way! Many of the parents I have worked with have battled to digest this idea. Out of love, they keep scanning their family life, looking for reasons and causes to explain their child's fragility. If something bad has happened or is happening to your child, you need to address it. But if hunting for causes doesn't get you past guess work, then shed the guilt and take your child as she is. We all carry dreams for our children, so perhaps this kind of acceptance may leave you feeling sad for a while. Take heart. This stance comes with some real advantages.

- You can accept (and enjoy) who your child is right now.
- You can help your child begin to understand and manage her emotions as they are happening.
- You can help your child to recognise and fulfil her unique potential.

It is very important for sensitive children to learn how to accept and manage their emotions in a challenging world. This enables growth. Growth starts from *where your child is* whilst change makes us dwell on *how we'd prefer things to be*. An approach based on growth is more respectful, realistic and, I think, more effective. It's much easier for a child to learn to manage her feelings than it is for anyone to try and make them vanish. While I do think that parents should protect growing children from much of the world's harshness; things are really going to get out of hand if you keep trying to change parts of the world to suit your children.

Conversations for Change

To illustrate, consider the child who gets distressed whenever her parents try to leave her with a babysitter. It's natural to want to try and make the distress go away. Here are some possibilities:

- We can spend a lot of time reassuring our child (that she is going to be safe, that the dinner won't take long). These are attempts to *change how a child feels*.
- We can tell our child that she's being a real pain; that she needs to grow up. This is an attempt to *change the child*.

- We can take our child with us and reroute to the local burger joint. This is an attempt to *change the child's world* into a place where parents never leave their children.

I understand these reactions. You love your child and it's horrible when she's distressed. But if you're working with a sensitive child, you're going to run into real problems if you keep trying to change her or her world so that she'll stop getting upset. For one thing, you'll find that the problem won't go away, it'll mutate. Once you've sorted out the 'nights out' problem, you could easily find that your child has found something new to fuss about! Secondly, (and here's my main concern) your child won't really have learnt anything.

It's natural for us to try and help sensitive children to become less sensitive. Studies show that children usually do learn to manage their emotions better as they get older. Over time most children get used to the everyday challenges of life. They get tougher. But, as parents, we have to be careful of our attempts to fast-track this process. Our efforts can easily give a child the idea that she is just not good enough; that she somehow has to change herself and toughen up if she is going to fit in and be blessed. In essence I am proposing the exact opposite: that strength and progress will flow as our children learn more about who they are as sensitive people. This evolving self-knowledge is almost exclusively generated within loving, patient, respectful relationships, relationships in which guilt-free adults enable a child to be open to her experiences and thoughts.

Quite often, parents will tell me that they find their sensitive children exhausting. I think this happens because we are pouring our energy into something that we can't really control: keeping our children in the zone of contentment. Of course we have a massive influence on our children's well-being, but at the end of the day, their emotions belong to them. We can only really control the way we respond to their experiences. We must aim to be good barrels, no matter how quirky the wine.

Conversations for Growth

Over time, just about every parent I've worked with has ended up taking a stance that's captured by the phrase: *"I'm sorry you feel that way..."* These loving people have tried, sometimes for years, to reassure their sensitive children past their upsets. And, by golly, they've made every effort to bypass all sorts of situations that they know are going to cause their children some distress. It hasn't worked. Life is just too complex, and it keeps on coming at us. Eventually, parents have found themselves saying things like:

> *"I know you don't want to do your homework. I'm sorry you feel that way"*

or

> *"I know that you're cross with me because I won't phone your friend for you. I'm sorry that you feel that way."*

Often parents add a 'but' to the phrase:

> *"I know that you're angry with me and that you get nervous when Dad and I go out. But sweetheart, Dad and I also need time together and I need you to help us. I know you can do it."*

It's not that these parents have suddenly stopped caring, or that they've given up on their children. It's just that they've realised, from experience, which whirlpools to avoid. Instead, children are asked to stop, think about their emotions, and make choices; actions that are vital for growth.

When your child is embarrassing

I guess most parents can remember a time when their child made them cringe, whether it's the supermarket tantrum or the loud and naively inappropriate comment about some poor, unsuspecting by-stander.

But sensitive children often have a particular knack for doing some really odd things. I think that we parents need to reflect on the ways that this makes us feel and act, especially when we're around other people. There's a good chance that you will feel a bit embarrassed about the way your sensitive child acts in certain situations. I think that's pretty normal, but we have to be careful. We give our children a potent sense of inadequacy if our embarrassment causes us to treat them differently when we're in certain company. Perhaps our tone of voice becomes more clipped. Perhaps we say things to them that we actually want the surrounding adults to hear. If we are honest with ourselves, I think we can admit that we do these things to save ourselves from our own awkwardness, and not for the benefit of our children.

My eight year old son has zero interest in sport. He does, on the other hand, love Yu-Gi-Oh cards. I do wish things were the other way around. Last Saturday we went to the mall because he was desperate to add the latest mini-pack to his collection. As we were about to enter the toy shop, we bumped into a sometimes friend of mine who, by my definition, is a "man's man". After a few small talk jokes he asked what we were up to. I pulled a face and made a dismissive comment about going in to purchase some "silly stuff".

I can still remember the confusion in my son's eyes as he looked up at me. I have noticed that he is now more reticent about his enthusiasm. I still don't know what to say to him about the cards.

The thing is, even if they're unable to say it, our children know when we do this. They know that they are embarrassing us and they often feel nothing short of dreadful.

If, like me, you sometimes find yourself bowing to these social pressures, use the table below to pinpoint when, where and with whom you might be most vulnerable to these mini-betrayals. By contrast, who helps you to feel most understood and supported as a parent of a sensitive child?

With Friends	With Family and In-Laws
....	....
....	....
....	....
....	....
....	....
General Public	**School Community**
....	....
....	....
....	....
....	....
....	....

How could you stand by your child more obviously the next time you're in the company of people who seem to frown at your child?

Next time I will ...

....

....

....

....

....

"To have faith (in another person) requires courage, the ability to take a risk, the readiness even to accept pain and disappointment."

– Erich Fromm –

Chapter 4

Recognise your child's temperament

Learn to read your child's arousal patterns

As almost any parent with more than one child can tell you, children are born different. Sometimes we can't believe that they were produced by the same factory! It's not just that our children often look different from each other, it's that their infant selves can be poles apart. A significant part of this difference can be attributed to *temperament*. Temperament has a lot to do with a child's nature, disposition or, if you like, personality.

Temperament can also be understood as a person's *inborn patterns of arousal*. When our children were born, my wife and I found ourselves choosing certain songs or tunes that somehow seemed to match who they were. As you think about your children, you are probably able to do the same. By our natures, some of us might spin around to the frenetic tempo of a fandango, whereas others of us are lucky enough to ease along to the smooth sounds of reggae.

Thomas and Chess (1981) were among the first researchers to study individual differences in infants' behaviour. They came up with nine 'dimensions' of temperament. To help you reflect on your child's inner experiences, use the following table to describe some of your child's infant tendencies (as you remember them, perhaps). For those of you with older children and teens, how would you say that these tendencies have evolved over the years? Next, imagine the temperament items in an adult context. How would you describe yourself on this table? How about the rest of your family?

Activity level. Some children crackle with energy whilst others are more placid and quiet.

....

....

Physical rhythms. Some infants sleep and eat at regular times, and you can even predict when to reach for a fresh nappy. Other babies like to keep everyone guessing.

....

....

Approach and avoidance. Some babies love to explore their worlds and they are stimulated by new sights and sounds. Then there are those who prefer to keep to what they know, thank you very much!

....

....

Adaptability. Adaptable babies are the ones who get forgotten as they lie peacefully snoozing near the bakery section at the local supermarket. They even forgive you afterwards.

....

....

Reactivity. As an infant, one of my children bawled loud and long when I leapt up to shout at the team on the TV screen. For the next hour, neither he nor my team took any advice from me.

....

....

Intensity. Some children experience big, cumulus nimbus-like emotions that dominate their experience. Others are born with a kind of mild diplomacy: "Oh by the way Mum, would you mind feeding me?"

....

....

Mood. Some babies are born with an overflow of chuckles. Others have an innate sense of the more sombre side of life *(Note: many therapists prefer not to define children according to this trait, because they point out that a child's mood is so dependent on context and upbringing).*

....

....

Distractibility. Some babies are happy for you to offer alternatives, whilst others want what they want. You may as well try to re-route the Amazon.

....

....

Attention span. When they play, some children like to finish what they start, whilst others are capable of exhausting a butterfly. I know which one I'd prefer to go shopping with.

....

....

Importantly, Harvard psychologist Jerome Kagan (2004) talks about children with *high reactivity* temperaments: children who are easily agitated, or aroused, by the unfamiliar. Comprising an estimated 15-20% of the population, these are the babies who are vulnerable to being emotionally oversensitive, cautious and perhaps anxious in later years.

Although the influence of temperament tends to blend into the complex fabric of a person's life, it's fascinating to notice how durable the strands can be. Many sensitive people say that, in one way or another, they've always been sensitive. They're just wired that way. This can be a rather painful realisation for us parents, particularly if your child is lurching from one emotional crisis to another. However, recognising and working with your child's temperament helps you to honour him as he is rather than as whom you wish he could be. Like a finger print, our arousal patterns are such an intimate component of who we are and how we experience our worlds. As such, your grand task now becomes to help your child learn how to manage himself according to his temperament rather than forcing him to behave in ways that go against his deeper nature. Some parents, with all the best intentions in the world, push their children into activities that they hope will make them emotionally tougher, not realising that these contrived events can promote self-doubt rather than social competence.

Although we might admire the way a naturally calm and happy child seems to cruise contentedly through life, I don't believe that there's such thing as a 'bad temperament'. Where would we be without the creativity and perceptiveness of the sensitive people that have walked the earth? And we need to nurture and develop the determination and zest that many intense children have.

I also need to emphasise that temperament patterns do not *determine* your child's emotional future. For instance, in his studies, Kagan found that by seven years of age, many of the high-reactive children had become significantly less fearful of life's challenges, primarily because they had secure and supportive homes. Temperament makes an important contribution to your child's lived experience, but it does not override many other environmental factors that are critical to your child's development.

How do you work with your child's temperament? Well for starters, *you* need to be finely tuned to the ways *you* are emotionally aroused when you are with your child. You might need to reflect on the ways that your own temperament interacts with your child. As distinct melodies, how well do they harmonise? Staying personally aware helps you to stay calm; and staying calm keeps you creative rather than reactive. You can stay focussed on the emotional lessons that your child needs to learn. It's very hard to contain and advise your child if you are in an emotional spin yourself.

Managing yourself

Remember, you are the first person to give order and meaning to your child's experiences. You give his sensations names and you are pivotal in categorising them as good or bad. So, in the heat of the battle, I want you to get past your habitual reactions of, guilt, irritation or despair. This can be deceptively difficult. As the parent of a sensitive child, you are probably going to feel *helpless* at times. No one likes that!

Breathe, relax, and start to focus your attention on your child's *real-time experience*. Look at him in terms of his arousal patterns. Don't try and solve the problem immediately. Take a precious moment to really notice your child. What is he experiencing in the situation? Children display high arousal in all sorts of ways, and we need to recognise that. Before seeing your sensitive child as nerdy or anxious, see him as emotionally aroused. Before seeing your child as embarrassingly shy, see him as emotionally aroused. Before seeing your child as naughty or difficult, see him as emotionally aroused. I feel particularly for children who get angry and intense when aroused. They're difficult to handle, because the more distressed they get the more combative they become. If we misread the signs, we can end up coming down harder and harder on a child who desperately needs to be soothed!

How to spot emotional arousal

There are many ways that children show that they are emotionally aroused. Here are some of the more common signs. You might like to tick off those that apply to your child:

☐ shallow breathing from the chest
☐ nervous movements with the arms or hands
☐ dropped head
☐ bunched and stooped shoulders
☐ avoidance of eye contact
☐ red face
☐ tense mouth or sucking on lips

☐ tears

☐ over-excited, naughty behaviour

☐ anger and resistance

☐ change in voice (pitch heightens)

As you watch your child, are there any other signs that you could add?

....

....

....

....

Learning to read your child's arousal barometer enables you to connect with him at any given moment. You know where his 'self' is occupied, so you are better able to join, guide and direct him through the hot spots and beyond. By contrast, if you ignore or dismiss your child's temperamental style you will frequently miss or misinterpret his actual lived experience, and your influence on his life is likely to be jarring and haphazard.

To illustrate, here's the kind of situation that some parents have described to me over the years:

Nicholas is just plain embarrassing when it comes to meeting adults whom he doesn't know! I was in the shops with him and a friend came up to chat. When she turned to Nicholas, he went all pathetic! He wouldn't look at her, he mumbled out some nonsense to her questions and then he drifted off to another aisle. I felt angry and awkward, and apologised to my friend. What do I do?

This is where an awareness of your child's arousal patterns is vital. If we don't recognise that our children are acting like this primarily because they feel emotionally uncomfortable, then we could easily address this as a problem of manners, and castigate them for being rude. This will only make the incident more emotionally complex for them, because they will feel bad about feeling bad. I'm not suggesting that manners don't count, far from it. But what I am saying is that a sensitive child will learn better if we first recognise that this social challenge (meeting unfamiliar people) is emotionally difficult. From here, because we have acknowledged our child's reality, we can then guide him with concrete suggestions that make emotional sense to him:

"Nicholas, I know that meeting new adults can make you nervous. But sweetheart, even though it's difficult I want you to practise being polite by looking up at their faces and trying to smile. The next time we're at the shops, I'll put my arm on your shoulder to remind you to relax and do these two things. Have I explained that clearly? Do you want to practise with me? Thank you for agreeing to try and for making me so proud."

I've known some sensitive children who, when they encounter an enthusiastic adult, will turn away and sometimes even walk away! Many indignant adults interpret this as insolence and all kinds of unnecessary upset can result. We have to show our children how to anticipate and cope with their arousal in these situations. Even sensitive adults tell me that their attempts to cope with social unease have sometimes given other people the impression that they are unfriendly, aloof, or even arrogant.

Of course, even if your child has a particular temperament, he's still one of a kind. With the billions of people who have gone before, and all those who are to follow, it's staggering to realise that there has never been another child exactly like yours and, furthermore, that there never will be another!

"Genuine conversation ... means acceptance of otherness"

– (Martin Buber) –

Chapter 5

The amazing changing brain

Understanding the brain can help you to manage yourself and your child.

I have to confess that I'm not all that comfortable in the world of biology, especially when daunting words like *prefrontal cortex* and *amygdala* are thrown at me. But in recent years I've found myself increasingly drawn to the exciting things that are being discovered about the brain. I think that some of these new findings have special relevance to the emotional lives of sensitive children.

Just as an aside, did you know it's estimated that there are more potential neural connections in your brain than there are atoms in the universe (Adler, H., 1995)? Now that deserves some serious respect!

Our brains are the last of our organs to mature fully. Some researchers suggest that the prefrontal cortex, which helps us to manage our emotional impulses, is only fully developed by the time we reach our early twenties. A person's social and emotional environment strongly influences neural development throughout this time. In other words, your everyday childhood experiences profoundly shape the way your adult brain works. This means that the way you and your child manage his sensitivity is likely to have long-lasting consequences!

However, it seems that our brains remain open to change throughout our lives. We used to have the idea that the brain was a fixed entity; that once your brain has formed, you have to live within its limitations. Current researchers have pretty much discounted this idea. The brain is, in fact, wonderfully designed to adapt and grow through the years. The brain is able, literally, to rewire itself in response to changing circumstances. Not only does this mean that your child will be able to change the way she responds, but so will you!

From the womb, we learn to think in a certain ways through patterns of interconnecting neurons called *neural networks*. As your child experiences new things, her brain works to make sense of all the data. Each thought or reaction stimulates a neural network in her brain and patterns, or pathways, start to form. Tiny electric pulses travel down these pathways connecting different parts of her brain. If the same neural pathway is repeatedly activated, it becomes automatic or habitual over time.

Emotions and the brain

Emotions are fundamental to brain functioning. They are said to co-ordinate, or integrate the different parts of the brain and give us an overall sense of meaning and direction. Because of the way the brain is structured, emotions activate our systems long before (in brain time) we can stop and think about what's happening. That's why arguing with an emotional child doesn't get us very far, while her emotional brain is buzzing there's very little space for logic.

Fear

The *amygdala* is an almond-shaped structure found deep in our brains. In fearful situations, it plays a key role in triggering the body's alarm system. Kagan's studies found that this part of the brain is more reactive in sensitive children. I've often found that it can help if a sensitive child understands that her internal alarm system tends to over-react. This system sends a lot of adrenaline (and other stress hormones) through her body when she's stressed. It helps her to understand how her emotions work and to feel more normal about some of her more difficult emotional and physical reactions.

When a sensitive child feels threatened or stressed, her adrenal system floods her body with adrenaline and stress hormones. Her breathing quickens, her heart races, muscle groups tense and digestion slows down. Blood flow is directed away from the major organs, to the muscles, in preparation for *flight or fight*. This is why you are not going to succeed in a rational argument with your emotional child: her body is more prepared to run or to fight than it is to think! This is also why sensitive children often have stomach or digestion problems!

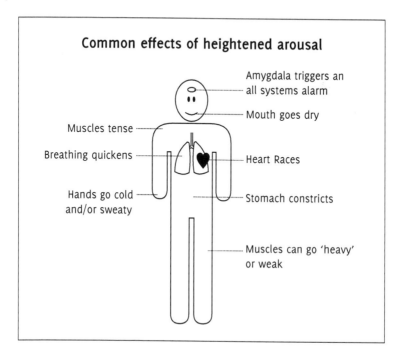

Common effects of heightened arousal

Amygdala triggers an all systems alarm

Mouth goes dry

Muscles tense

Breathing quickens

Hands go cold and/or sweaty

Heart Races

Stomach constricts

Muscles can go 'heavy' or weak

Fear tends to be an overbearing emotion. Our bodies are designed to react to a threat with speed and intensity. We don't do a lot of thinking when we're in danger. This is a good thing. Thoughtfulness doesn't count for much when a crocodile is sizing up one of your limbs. Once our brains have identified something as dangerous, it takes quite a bit of convincing for us to change our minds. The problem, of course, is that so many of the things that trigger our fear reactions (fight, flight, or freeze) are symbolic. They are dangerous because of what they mean to us. A birthday party is normally low on the list of community hazards, but not for a person who believes that she is stupid and that she will make a fool of herself before the first game begins.

Sensitive children are often fearful in situations that we see as non-threatening. We're left amazed and probably exasperated when our children get upset without any apparent reason. While the rest of the family rushes off to enjoy a morning at the circus, your sensitive child won't even get out of the car.

Learning new habits

However, the brain is able to grow and adapt. Research shows that new habits of thought and behaviour can actually change the brain chemistry of people who struggle with intense anxiety difficulties (Schwartz, et. al., 1996). If, over time, we enable our child to practise a new thought or action deliberately, the pattern of her arousal reactions can change in some profound ways. As Daniel Siegel argues, "Connections in the brain shape the way you think, but the flip side is true too ... The way you think can change your brain. Neural firing changes neural connections – if you pay attention." (p.37, 2004)

So, how do we help a sensitive child to 'pay attention' when she's overwhelmed by unhelpful emotions? Anything that helps your child to boost her inner awareness, despite the influence of intoxicating emotions, can kick-start the new learning. Techniques that promote self-awareness and control; such as naming the feeling (p.52-54), breathing exercises (p.46-47), muscle relaxation (p.48-50), focus thoughts (p.89-91, 109) and deliberate actions (p.90-92, and Chapter 11) are all useful possibilities.

The triune brain

Neuroscientist Paul MacLean suggests that the brain consists of three intricately connected areas. The brain stem, which is primarily *reactive* in nature, functions beyond our conscious awareness, controlling such aspects as our balance, our breathing and our heartbeat. The second area; the limbic system, regulates the brain stem and plays a critical role in our experience of emotions. MacLean says that the limbic system helps us rapidly to identify events as either 'agreeable' or 'disagreeable'. We are powerfully primed to avoid the things that feel bad and seek out the things that feel good. The third area, the neocortex, enables reflection, reasoning, and the ability to use words to describe these complex thoughts. The words themselves give us a sense of distance or perspective on our experiences, so promoting flexibility and choice.

The front part of our brains, the prefrontal cortex, helps us to be aware of our emotions, to manage them and to make thoughtful choices. It enables us to override unhelpful emotional impulses (Goleman, Boyatzis & McKee, 2002). Interestingly, studies show that the prefrontal cortex develops through our relationships with others. As children, we learn vital lessons of emotional regulation and wisdom through our interactions with our parents and other role models. Thankfully, it seems that it continues to evolve throughout our lives. We are never too old to develop emotional wisdom.

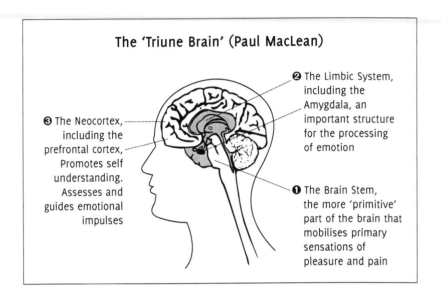

The 'Triune Brain' (Paul MacLean)

❷ The Limbic System, including the Amygdala, an important structure for the processing of emotion

❸ The Neocortex, including the prefrontal cortex, Promotes self understanding. Assesses and guides emotional impulses

❶ The Brain Stem, the more 'primitive' part of the brain that mobilises primary sensations of pleasure and pain

You carry your child's emotions

Emotions are contagious! Our brains have what are called *mirror neurons* which help us to read and anticipate other people's thoughts, actions and feelings. Because they reflect what others feel, mirror neurons enable us to see things from another person's perspective. This means that your body is going to echo your child's distress. You will not be emotionally or physically neutral when your child is in a spin (Stern, 2004). How you cope with this is very important Because your child has her own mirror neurons, she will be influenced by the ways you handle the overall emotions of the situation. Your ability to act as a container for the emotions helps your child to feel soothed. So how you respond to, and guide your child's emotional experiences makes a big difference to her inner experience.

> **Try this!**
>
> As you look to guide your children, practise these three things:
>
> ❶ Be aware of your own feelings
>
> ❷ Identify and acknowledge your child's feelings
>
> ❸ At the same time, stay in control.

It's not always easy. But this combination of contrasts gives your child a small taste of self-regulation because in that moment her brain and body are calmed and coached by the integrated, relaxed rhythms of your brain and body.

Daily practice

When it comes to learning new habits, the brain responds well to repetition. Apparently this is especially so if we want to tackle our *emotional* habits (Goleman, Boyatzis & McKee, 2002). So hang on to a mixture of patience and diligence. Each time you help your child to acknowledge but contain her emotions, she improves her ability to self-regulate. It's an intimate, everyday, neural network-building dance. And, of course, new neural habits are strengthened each time your child remembers to focus her thoughts on more positive, con-structive truths about herself and her world.

Challenges and threats

Our arousal system reacts differently to *challenges* and *threats*. A challenge arouses us in a 'good' way. We feel in control, we feel posi-tive and excited and we are focussed. After the event, we feel ener-gised and strong. On the other hand, threats arouse us in 'bad' ways.

We feel tense and we are distracted by the harm that we might suffer. After the event we are likely to feel drained and even a bit down. I often think about these two energy patterns when I'm helping a child to set goals (see *Teach your child to focus on what he can control*, p.136). Because of its positive effects, I want sensitive, hard-working children to be motivated by *challenging* goals as much as possible. And because sensitive children often feel threatened by unfamiliar situations, I want them to learn how to break these stressful moments down into step-by-step, controllable challenges.

....

Science is uncovering many fascinating insights into the workings of our brains. As a non-scientist, I realise again that it definitely pays to keep in touch with our feelings, that our daily experiences and interactions are crisply configured by the ebb and flow of our emotions. And then I also have a renewed sense of hope in the empowering and restorative properties of relationships.

"Parents are the active sculptors
of their children's growing brains."

– (Siegel & Hartzell) –

Chapter 6

Help your child to stay connected to his body

When we become more 'present-centred'
we are able to make choices in the moment

There are two very good reasons to teach your child to become aware of the ways that arousal affects her body. For one thing, if she is more aware of how she tenses up in certain situations, she will be able to use this knowledge as an excellent early warning sign when she's practising emotional self-control.

Secondly, knowing how to relax can help your child to recover better at the end of a stressful day. It's amazing how physically disconnected most of us are, and how we store muscular tension for large portions of our lives, without ever realising it. And because it seems as though the world is only getting more stressful, we need to teach our children to relax and let go of their tension regularly. Can you imagine how a sensitive child might stockpile physical stress during a tough school day? Without a way to release this tension your child may become more and more 'strung out' inside.

"Judy is just unplayable when she gets tired! Nowadays we know what signs to look out for and when she comes home spitting lightning bolts, we just try to get her through the evening and into bed with as little fuss as possible."

It's worth remembering that sensitive children are often stressed by things that may pass well below our radars (Aron 2002). Believe it or not, quite a few sensitive children have told me that they feel happier in cold, gloomy weather and darkened rooms; that warm, sunny days tend to be too full of brightness and bustle. So, whether it's busy days, loud people, or subtle changes in routine, realise that the world may contain hidden stressors for your child. Paying attention to the things that tax your child's inner peace will help you to better guide him in his own self-management.

There are many ways to relax and it makes sense for individuals to develop their own style. Each one of us tends to tense up in habitual, repetitive ways that we need to recognise. Notice your child's posture. How does it change when he gets tense? How is his behaviour affected by tension? Are there any physical complaints (e.g. headaches or sore tummies) to give you some clues about where he might be storing tension? Use the diagram alongside to shade in those areas of your child's body that seem to hold tension.

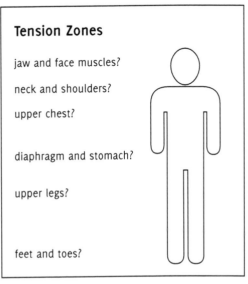

Tension Zones

jaw and face muscles?

neck and shoulders?

upper chest?

diaphragm and stomach?

upper legs?

feet and toes?

Remember that, because emotions are contagious, you and your child will already share patterns of physical arousal. When he starts to get tense, your body will have its own particular echo, and vice versa. Now here's the point; if you (and, over time, your child) can start to become more aware of your shared arousal, you will have a chance to communicate more creatively with each other. You will be more able to intercept and change bad and unhelpful habits. It's not that your bodies will necessarily feel any different, but you will be more able to choose what you do with those feelings. Instead of getting sucked into repetitive yelling matches, or impulsive rescuing, you can slow down and act with more insight.

Relaxation

Because we are so used to being tense, being able to relax often takes some practise. But the benefits are clear. Developing this skill enhances a sense of poise and self-control and, because we become more 'present-centred' we are able to make choices in the moment.

I try to teach children fairly simple, quick ways to relax, mainly because these can be used at any time of the day. Also, my goal is that children learn how to *regulate* their arousal. Getting children to wander around in some sort of zombie-like state of relaxation is not the point. *On-going* tension is bad, rather than tension itself. I sometimes ask children to imagine a tap inside them. When they are feeling very stressed or worried, the tap is turned on too far. By breathing properly and by relaxing key muscles, they can turn the tap back to a more comfortable flow (but not off).

Recognising tension

Work through the following steps to see whether your child knows the difference between tense and relaxed muscles.

- Ask your child to describe the different feelings as he clenches and then relaxes one of his hands. Ask him to describe other muscle groups in his body that he can tense and relax in this way.

- Ask him to describe other muscles in his body that he can also tense up. Explain what tension is.

- Extend the experience by asking your child to imagine that he is becoming a floppy rag doll, as first his shoulders; then his arms and then his legs become loose and relaxed. Ask him about the two different feelings. Listen to the words that he uses, because these words can become a part of your own private vocabulary for managing tension.

Breathing for calmness

Once children know what relaxation feels like, I encourage them to practise breathing from the diaphragm (long, slow tummy breathing) whilst relaxing their chests and shoulders. The following steps will help you to introduce this skill to your child.

- Ask him to lie down, place a toy on his solar plexus and another on his chest. He can practise the two different ways of breathing as he watches either toy go for a breath ride (tummy breath versus chest breath).

- Once he can do the different breathings easily, practise it in a standing position. Place your hand just below his rib cage and encourage him to relax and breathe from this place.

- Younger children have enjoyed imagining that they are kangaroos with a joey in the pouch, and they have to rock the joey to sleep with their breathing.

Some children who have just started this exercise say that this part of their body is sore from all the tension it's been carrying! As you might see from these examples, I make quite a fuss about tummy breaths as I think that they are an important part of self-management. I quite often say to children that a good, deep tummy breath gives them the chance to change the DVD in their heads from worried or gloomy thoughts to realistic or positive thoughts.

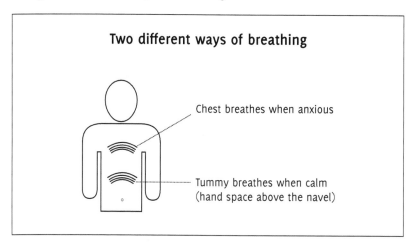

Two different ways of breathing

Chest breathes when anxious

Tummy breathes when calm
(hand space above the navel)

So what's so bad about chest breathing?

When we get stressed or worried, we tend to take quick, shallow breaths, drawing our breath from our chests rather than our diaphragms (the dome-shaped muscle at the bottom of our lungs). Now, because only the upper part of our lungs fills with air; we aren't able to take in a full quota of oxygen. Because less oxygen is now being circulated through the bloodstream, a warning alarm is triggered in the brain releasing *even more* adrenaline into our systems. This serves to raise our anxiety, our shallow breathing continues and our adrenaline levels remain elevated. Unwittingly, we find ourselves caught in a vicious cycle (Reivitch & Shatte, 2002).

Changing posture

Next, I suggest to children that they imagine hanging their shoulders onto a nicely curved clothes hanger, so that they drop into a more natural, relaxed shape. They can practise this in front of a mirror. Once a child has the idea, you can encourage him to practise the combined skills of relaxing muscles, breathing for calmness and noticing his posture by drawing an 'X' on his hand. Each time he notices the X during the day, it should remind him to relax.

If you and your younger child have developed an understanding, simply placing a hand on his shoulders can be a signal to him to notice that he is getting tense and that he needs to take some good breaths and relax. This signal is usefully discrete when you and your child are in the company of others.

Body comfort

Tragically, many sensitive children dislike their physical selves. Please don't underestimate this more subtle version of body tension. Typically during adolescence, but sometimes even earlier, some children feel unhappy with their bodies. Although girls are often the victims of this internal war, many boys are getting caught up in the battle too. Sad! Although it's beyond the scope of this book, stay vigilant to the cultural lies that tell our children that they aren't acceptable if they aren't thin or muscular. Thin legs or not, six pack or not, can your child romp on the beach? Does she stand tall? Is he comfortable in his body? Are you?

Teaching relaxation

• For younger children (3-10)

When I show a child how to relax, I try to keep the exercise fairly short and I certainly don't force the issue. Relaxation and effort just don't go together! Also, I don't think it helps to be too serious when you are teaching a child about relaxation. You'll probably get laughed at if you start using some kind of solemn, hypnotic voice! Your child might like to squirm about, or ask questions, or make comments. Let him. I usually tell a child that he may be able to concentrate better when he closes his eyes, but some children don't like to do this and I don't insist on it. Partner your child in these exercises, praise his efforts and be responsive to his ideas and suggestions about how relaxation works.

Remember that young children often respond very quickly during relaxation exercises, so you don't need to draw things out. When a child's happy to sit down for a while, I start by talking about the difference between a tummy breath and a chest breath. For me, this is central. And, as I've said above, another of my main goals is to give children an idea of the difference between muscle tension and relaxation.

With younger children I often say the following:

"Pretend that you are Raggedy Ann (Andy), floppy all over, loose and comfortable. Let's be like Raggedy Ann and feel all floppy. Let me check this arm. Good. See how it flops down when I pick it up. Just like Raggedy Ann. Now let me check the other arm. Good! That's nice and floppy too. Now let yourself feel floppy all over, loose all over, and very comfortable all over; you can be floppy Raggedy Ann."

• For older children

I often take older children through a more complete relaxation exercise, which teaches them more about the different muscle groups in their bodies, and the ways that they might be habitually tense. It goes something like this:

"Notice your breathing. Breathe in relaxation, and breathe out tension. Now let this relaxed, warm feeling move through from your chest and tummy muscles, down through your hips and upper leg muscles. Now relax your lower leg muscles and, as you breathe out from your tummy, let the relaxing feeling go on down to your ankles, feet and toes. Let the warm feelings flow in a comfortable way. You're doing really well! Now think about your lower back muscles, and loosen them. Now let the relaxed feelings move into your upper back muscles; past your nicely relaxed shoulders, down into the upper arms, slowly past the elbows and into your lower arm muscles. Now let the good, warm feeling move into the small muscles of your wrists, hands and even into the little muscles of your fingers. Great! When you're ready, let your neck muscles relax a bit more. Feel how your head is comfortably balanced. Now ... as the relaxed feelings spread, just let your jaw get nice and loose ... and then let this nice, comfortable feeling spread into your forehead, around your eyes and into your scalp. Feel nice and comfortable all over. Great stuff!"

If your child responds to this or some other version of progressive muscle relaxation, let him know that he will get even better with practice. Encourage him to make it a part of his daily, or evening routine.

I've seen a few anxious teenagers who just don't like these kinds of exercises. The idea of closing their eyes and trying to relax different muscles only seems to make them feel less in control and more anxious! So again, I am careful to stick to what works for teenagers. I might ask them to describe the things that do leave them feeling more relaxed and we develop something more personally suitable from there. Even as I stay within their personal preferences, my aim is still to leave these teens with some portable ways of relaxing or focusing themselves 'in the moment'. A sixteen-year old found that he had a habit of scrunching up his toes when he felt stressed. We built on this habit by using this as a cue to breathe from the diaphragm and relax his shoulders.

Busy children

Many sensitive children are prone to over stimulation. Unwittingly, they secrete high levels of stress hormones (adrenaline and nor adrenaline) during the course of a busy day: bio-chemicals that can have a big influence on their emotional and physical well-being. However, it's the *duration* of stimulation, or stress, that's harmful to our children, rather than the stress itself. That's why we have to be so careful of days filled with wall-to-wall activity. As parents, we need to be aware that our children can easily get seduced by this social hazard. Where necessary, be brave enough to say 'no' to the rich diet of structured activities that can so easily clog up our days.

Over the past two years Kerry has begun to take her studies extremely seriously and she is capable of working late into the night. Now that she's in her final year, she has sharpened her focus even more and she has set herself wonderfully high goals for the end-of-year exams. Kerry's problem is that she often feels like she's running on adrenaline. Her mind is still racing when she turns from her books to put her head on the pillow and she's battling to get to sleep. Her whole body feels 'wired'. As she tries to go to sleep, she ends up worrying about the fact that she can't which only makes things worse!

Sensitive children are often more emotionally fragile when they're tired. Consequently, many parents find that it's really important to give their sensitive children some 'cool down' time at the end of a school day. For some children, this might mean playing quietly for a while, or reading, or jumping on a trampoline. One mum told us that she sometimes gives her child a soothing bath if he comes home ashen faced and wild eyed. You need to look out for end-of-the-day involvements that don't keep your child focussed on any serious *goals*. Perhaps it's unnecessary to say this, but homework, piano practise and swimming training don't always carry the physical and emotional relief that every child needs. Remember, growth happens when we alternate between exertion and rest.

What if it doesn't work?

It's important to know that when your child is very anxious and upset, tummy breaths and relaxed shoulders will hardly seem to help at all! It's actually very difficult to move oneself from an anxious state to a calm state. But don't discard the principles. Staying in touch with one's physical self, and knowing how to relax, are quiet, internal skills that can contribute to your child's emotional health for years to come.

"The brain looks to the body to know how it feels and to assess the meaning of things"

– (Siegel & Hartzell) –

Chapter 7

Find a way to talk to your child about her feelings

Good moments contain the seed of hopeful futures

Emotions prompt so much of what we say and do, yet we seldom stop to talk about these powerful undercurrents. If you have a sensitive child it's really important to get him used to talking about his feelings. It can be surprisingly tricky. Emotional meltdowns tend to leave everyone in the vicinity feeling awkward. Many of us instinctively try to get back to calmer waters as quickly as possible, which means that we don't say much about what just happened. When I talk to a sensitive child about his emotional difficulties, I often find that he starts to tense up and, because he doesn't know what words to use, to close up. Often there are tears, which is understandable. But if a child is experiencing frequent emotional episodes and you want to help him to grow past these difficulties, you need to find a way to talk about the problem.

Our sensitive son can be terribly slow to warm up to things. Often, we just know that he would really enjoy something if he would just give it a try, but no Sir, he'll only come on board when he's well and truly ready. I remember one evening when he returned from an activity that all of us had been trying to persuade him to do for ages. He approached the car with a smile and a flushed face, excited by the fun he had just had and full of stories. Midway through his third story his sister turned to him and said, "Michael, you are 'green eggs and ham'". We all laughed, knowing that she was referring to that wonderful Dr Seuss story about a cat that keeps refusing to sample a meal of green eggs and ham only to discover that, in fact, it tastes delicious.

Well, that was a long time ago now. But ever since then we've been able to talk much more openly and effectively with Michael about how uncertain he sometimes feels, how he doubts himself, and his potentially negative habit of avoiding new things.

Start simple and then go for more detail

You don't have to approach your child's feelings with laser-like insight, able to read every nuance of his heart. In fact it's important for your child to learn, for himself, how to grasp his inner experience and put it into words. You do not have to be the expert. But you will give him opportunities to learn about his emotions if you simply notice when he's feeling 'bad' and give him a chance to talk more about it.

"Derek buddy, you don't look happy (basic emotion). *What's wrong?"* (look for context clues)

"Mom, I'm so over Maths. I really worked hard for my test but I only got 62%. Useless!"

(Mom takes in this information, giving herself a chance to get the feel of it.)

"Gee, that's so disappointing (specific label). *If I was you I'd probably feel so frustrated* (specific label). *Sorry babe".*

(As Mom gives Derek a chance to own and settle his feelings, she can find a time later in the day to circle back and talk about things like effort, pride, and staying positive.)

Finding the words to describe an emotional experience is, for me, one of the first ways that a child begins to get some control over her emotions. Giving a feeling a name, and talking about the ways that feeling manifests in her life, is strangely empowering, even though it can be difficult. It promotes understanding. The details of your child's experience are also fleshed out enough for you both to start thinking about new possibilities. With her new insights, she can become a *participant* in the creation of possible solutions and goals.

Often we can speak about the problem only when we're surrounded by it, and it's we parents who do all the talking. We ask our children why they do the things they do (unanswerable). Or we tell them that they shouldn't feel the way they're feeling (unanswerable). Or we tell them how much they're irritating us (unanswerable). There is no real dialogue, no reflective participation by our children. As a result, we end up relying on our powers of surveillance, interception and reassurance to keep the problem at bay. We struggle to move our children towards changes that they just don't understand and probably haven't agreed to. It's exhausting and it doesn't really work! For starters, children are unlikely to take real responsibility for changes that they haven't bought into. Also, because their own creative energy has been bypassed, children could easily become passive or even resistant to change. And, of course, there's every chance that your efforts to change your child are going to give her the subtle but unfortunately powerful message that she's not good enough as she is.

Reasons and Descriptions

When it comes to talking with children about their feelings, many parents only ask 'why' questions *(Why are you so upset? Why don't you want to go? Why are you scared?)*. Of course, it's important to know when something is troubling our children, because then we can try to fix it. But please don't forget about the value of 'what' questions *(What happened? What did it make you feel? What do you feel in your body?)*. Remember that sensitive don't always need much of a 'why' to feel highly emotional. And often, they don't really know why they are feeling upset. If we press our children for a valid reason, they can start to feel even worse and they'll probably make up any old reason just to put an end to our questions.

Remember, looking for external causes will often only get you so far with sensitive children. Most of the real work lies, not in fixing our children's worlds, but in helping them to understand and cope with their emotional experiences. Asking lots of 'what' questions helps your sensitive child to give you repeated descriptions of her inner experiences, and this knowledge is going to be really useful when she encounters other emotional challenges further down the road. Your effectiveness as a parent/coach will accumulate because she will almost certainly be experiencing a very similar cluster of emotions along the way. Her personal themes will start to emerge (e.g. fear of failure, fear of the 'spotlight', fear of being out of control). By contrast, the reasons for her upsets will be historically rooted. Whatever upset her at the age of five will be pretty irrelevant to her by the time she's twelve. At that level, everything changes.

'What' questions also enable our children to describe their inner experiences when they have managed to do something well *("Well done Sally, you played so nicely at the Finch's home. How did you do that? What did you do differently?")*

Children are more than their feelings

When we give our children a chance to look at and discuss their feelings, they get a chance to see that these emotions are only a part of who they are. It is an important part, sure, but still just a part. I love to borrow from an approach called *externalisation* (White & Epston, 1990) because it emphasises this so creatively. Externalisation protects the dignity of children. It helps them to explore their emotions. It mobilises their energy to change and it frees parents up to play a more light-hearted, supportive role. Here is an example:

Simon had a lousy Sunday. As a result, so had we. From about 6 a.m. he started grousing about the Church picnic happening later that morning. He complained about the other children and he reminded us (as if we needed it) just how much he hated the organised games that went with the occasion. We did our best to ignore him although I couldn't help muttering that he was a bloody pain. I also pointed out to him that his younger sister was really showing him up which, of course, did nothing to improve his mood.

The outing did not go well! Simon spent most of his time in the car. I lost it for a while and dragged him out when the others were playing soccer. I knew I was wrong even before my wife gave me a well deserved "You're an idiot" look. Simon returned to the car in tears and I really didn't know what to say to him after that.

Later that night I went to Simon's room and we started to talk. Following some much needed advice, I started by asking him what the day had been like for him. What had he been feeling? Simon started to cry. He told me that he had felt horrible inside all day, as though something bad was going to happen to him. He also said that he thought I preferred his sister to him and that I was disappointed in him because he wasn't good at sports. I suggested that these horrible feelings and thoughts could be called 'worry' and we started to think about the other times that 'worry' affected Simon's life. We took our time and even though he was upset it seemed as if Simon appreciated the chance to talk in this way.

I explained how frustrated I got when I felt like worry was over-powering him and I wondered how it was for Simon himself when these times came. Simon said that he also didn't like it but that he didn't know what to do because sometimes worry just seemed to take over. We agreed that we would look for ways that Simon could begin to deal with worry, to block the ways it seemed to be influencing his life.

I then started to remind Simon of times that he'd been brave, times when he'd done good things even though he felt a bit ner-vous. I said how proud I was of him; that he was the perfect son for me and that I was lucky to have him in my life. I did remember to apologise to my boy before I turned off the light.

Externalisation includes the following important steps:

• Step 1

Give your child's problem a name. Take your time over this, because the right name will come out of the conversations you have with her. She must feel that she has contributed to the name, and she must agree that it fits her own experiences.

• Step 2

Speak about the problem as being connected to, but separate from your child. So, instead of asking "Are you worried again?" you ask "Is Worry giving you a hard time again?"

• Step 3

Encourage your child to practise the skill of taking a stand despite feeling rotten: "I know it's horrible when worry makes you feel that way. Have you decided what you want to do about it?" It's her problem and she's responsible for developing new abilities that will help her to resist the unwanted feeling.

• Step 4

Focus on the exceptions: those times that your child has surprised you by her toughness in the face of challenges: "Well done my girl! I could see that you felt a bit nervous but you went ahead and helped your sister anyway". These exceptions provide your child with powerful alternative truths that need to be highlighted.

Once your child's relationship to the problem has been put in this way you are able to *partner* him by teaching him a range of anti-problem skills and by celebrating the progress that he makes.

Simon still has his bouts with worry but the way we deal with these times is very different. He's learnt to breathe and relax when he starts to feel tense and he practises holding sensible thoughts in his mind. During our discussions we started to work out better ways for Simon to act when he starts to feel tense. He now has something to aim for during these difficult times and he knows that we support him. I feel much more connected with him during his struggles and it's really great to be able to praise him when I can see that he is behaving bravely despite feeling horrible inside.

Separate the problem from the child

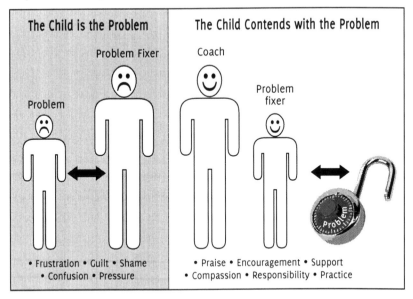

The Child is the Problem	The Child Contends with the Problem
Problem Fixer	Coach
Problem	Problem fixer
• Frustration • Guilt • Shame • Confusion • Pressure	• Praise • Encouragement • Support • Compassion • Responsibility • Practice

Some children just don't like speaking about their problems in the way I have just described, and I encourage you not to force the issue. Externalisation does tend to protect children's integrity (they are more than their problems and difficulties), but with that comes greater responsibility. Not all children will like that at first. Where appropriate, you may need to talk quite openly with your child about the fact that, while you're always there to encourage and support, he's really the only one who can overcome his emotional challenges. You can't defeat worry for him.

Regardless of how far you get with the process of externalisation, keep the basic principles in mind: name the problem; separate your child from the problem; practise taking a stand against the problem and focus on the successes. These principles help you to make every day, respectful responses to the difficulties that your child may be having:

"Well done, you didn't let self-doubt trip you up!"

"That sounds like Worry Bug talk to me."

"I hate it when frustration gets the better of you."

"Please bring helpful Mark back."

"There's that Ferrari engine of yours again! Take your foot off the pedal a bit, boy, and then I'll talk with you."

Externalisation demotes problem behaviour from the status of 'me' to the status of 'my choices'. Talking in this way with our children helps them to stay connected with their better selves, with the unrealised potential that they all have. You are showing your child that he is so much more than his fears, that his problems do not define him and that you respect his struggles with these problems.

But, of course, there are lots of other ways to talk to a child about her feelings. As I said earlier, I have found that many older children and teens respond well to explanations about the biology of arousal (the amygdala, adrenaline, and the way emotions and thoughts work in our brains). But still, even older children find it much easier to join me in the conversation when we use metaphors from their worlds.

My eighteen year-old, horse-riding daughter was going on again about something that had upset her and I was getting a very familiar sinking feeling inside. But then I started to get angry. I told her that it was as though her emotions were like a big, powerful horse that she had never learnt to ride. I said that I had always been worried that the big horse would hurt her and that was why I had held the reins up to now. But then I told my daughter how tired I was of feeling responsible, anxious and guilty every time she felt like she couldn't cope. I said that I loved her so much but that I really felt like it was time for her to learn how to control her own horse. Time for her, and, certainly, time for me. She was a bit angry with me at first, but I felt deeply that this change had to happen and, over time, she started to understand and agree. We still talk about the horse sometimes.

Because externalising separates the problem behaviour from the child, it becomes easier to highlight times when your child is not dominated by the problem. Many parents have told me how surprisingly strong, mature, cheerful and helpful their sensitive children can be. It's really critical to look out for and highlight these exceptions. Michael White encourages us to make the exceptions "sparkle". A wonderfully fresh wind blows when you begin actively to notice these perhaps unacknowledged moments. Because your attention means so much to your child, he will be motivated to repeat that behaviour. So you need to get to the stage where you can be calm when your child is upset, and excited and encouraging when he is showing good self-control.

Highlighting what you *do* want helps your child to clarify, understand and *sort* her emotional life. Glasser and Easley (2005) point out that "parents are essential in directing traffic in regard to their child's inner experience and choices, which are more or less likely to become experiences of success or failure, depending upon how they are viewed. The experience may not wind up in the right bin on its own. It needs sorting. That means help from you." (p.74)

A powerful way of helping your child see that you acknowledge her good parts is to practise some 'gossiping in the presence'. Look for a situation where she can overhear your praise. For example, when your daughter is in the vicinity, you might say to your husband "Nicky really enjoyed going to play with Jessie today! She almost forgot to say goodbye to me. She is getting so grown up!" She has just heard a story to offset the times when she acts overly shy or clingy.

As you draw attention to your child's good moments, she gets the opportunity to match key words with inner feelings and outer actions. You are giving her a real-life, immediate and personal example of the kinds of things you want her to do more often. She also realises that she is able to make good choices. Again, to quote Glasser and Easley, "If you focus on the smart, thoughtful or rule-related choices your child makes, she receives a success message about who she is as well as about her positive capabilities. It's almost as though we lend the experience our energy and wisdom. The loan eventually becomes an inheritance." (p.75) Good moments contain the seeds of hopeful futures. Make them vivid.

Our oldest child, Michael, is a sensitive boy. In so many ways he's just lovely, but his strong reactions can be difficult to manage. He went through a season where he was very cross with his younger brother and sister. He felt like they got away with too much and that we always blamed him when there was an altercation. In hindsight we probably did expect too much from him at that time. Although he is quite a bit older than his siblings, we have to keep reminding ourselves that he's still a child. Anyway, because he was upset, Michael used to lash out at his brother and sister when they got in his way. We would then blast him, which only made him more upset.

As parents, we decided to change gears from our side. When we saw that Michael was upset, we would try to understand how irritated he felt and to acknowledge how difficult it could be to be the oldest. We asked him to come and tell us when he was being bugged and we promised that we would try to help. We also actively started to look for those moments when Michael was sweet to his sister and brother, and to thank him for the way he was helping us. We started to say that his siblings were lucky to have a responsible older brother like him. We also started to give him special privileges for being the eldest (staying up a bit later, a particular seat in the car) and to reward him when he helped us with his responsibility. Michael is, of course, still a child, but it's been wonderful to see him stepping into the fresh role that this approach has created.

"We remember criticism,
but we respond to praise."

— Laura Roberts, et al. —

Chapter 8

Everyday talk

Our conversations can keep us stuck

Family conversations tend to follow invisible scripts. It's worth paying attention to these repetitive patterns because, in so many ways, they play a critical part in the health of family relationships. Whether it's planning for the holidays, settling the finances, or entertaining guests, we tend to slot into certain roles. Of course, we also adopt roles as we go about the task of parenting.

Now, unless we make the effort to step back for the occasional review, the 'rules' behind our family scripts can end up restricting us. If you are feeling stuck in your home relationships, it can be helpful to look at three things that happen each time people communicate with each other (Harre & Van Langenhove 1991).

- Each person takes up a certain 'role' in a conversation (e.g. I am the responsible one, or the helpless one, or the sensible one, or the emotional one).

- The flow of a conversation tends to have some history behind it. As we start to talk, we have the sense that we've been down this road before.

- Nevertheless, every conversation is also an opportunity to be creative.

So take a moment to reflect on the relationship that you and your sensitive child share. Of course, every relationship is allowed to have some ragged patches, but you might find that there's a particular corner that's becoming really toxic. Every time it happens, you feel frustrated, upset and stuck.

If you think about it, many of these everyday conversations involve other members of the family. So it can get quite complicated! For example, when your child doesn't want to do his homework (again), you find yourself moaning at him (again), and he says (again) that his younger sister always gets away with everything, and your husband comes in and asks what the problem is (again) and you feel guilty (again).

Try this!

Just to get you started, use the example provided to capture what happens when you and your partner approach a problem with your sensitive child. Naturally, there could be many other versions of family interaction that you might want reflect on.

❶ Child (starts to say and do ...)

....

....

❷ I (start to say and do ...)

....

....

❸ My partner (starts to say and do ...)

....

....

- What role are you playing? What roles are the others playing (remember that roles normally complement each other, e.g. the disciplinarian role and the compassionate role)?

- What historical events could be influencing each of you to take on these roles (e.g. your own family backgrounds, events surrounding pregnancy, or your child's early years)? Think carefully about this one!

....

....

....

....

- And now: what might a new, more creative conversation look like?

❶ Child (starts to say and do ...)

....

....

❷ I (start to say and do ...)

....

....

❸ My partner (starts to say and do ...)

....

....

There's nothing wrong with taking on a role in the family. In fact, it's perfectly natural. But I want you to listen to the way it makes you feel. If you are feeling miserable, you're probably stuck in a role that is unhealthy and limiting. The thing is, if it's not good for you, the chances are that it will be less than ideal for others in the family too.

Body Language

Do remember that much of our daily communication is non-verbal. In families, even the smallest of gestures, perhaps a frown, or certain smile or a sigh can carry influential local meaning. When you're parenting a sensitive child, it's tremendously helpful to get smart about these fleeting but powerful signals. Just for a moment, think about your child's emotional displays as forms of *communication*. What do you assume that your child is *saying* to you when he gets distressed? What's the unspoken message that you receive? Could it be something to do with your competence as a parent, or that your child is helpless and needs to be rescued?

What does your child do with his eyes, his arms, or the rest of his body when he's distressed? You might like to refer to the list of arousal signs in Chapter 4 to help you with this exercise. How do you tend to *interpret* those signals?

Now reflect on yourself for a moment. When you're feeling brave, ask someone else in your family to add what they have noticed about the ways your body commonly 'talks' during times of family distress. What messages do you send out to the rest of your family?

We are not normally aware of the unspoken signals that each of us gives off to those around us. But I am convinced that these messages are far more powerful than we realise. Taking the time to reflect on our body language can help us to stay close to some of the fundamental beliefs that we unconsciously hold about ourselves, our partners, and our children.

In the shadows of our words

Newspapers are scary things nowadays. There seem to be so many awful things going on. I don't know about you, but I can't think of a dinner party in the recent past, that hasn't given over a good portion of time to doom and gloom reflections and prophecies.

We have to watch for the kind of mindset that our moans and groans establish, both for ourselves and our children. Should we be surprised when intelligent children become troubled when they're fed with a steady diet of how bad things are getting? As I talk with children, I'm sometimes struck by how faithfully they mirror their parents' attitude to life. Almost word for word, they use the same phrases. How are you and your family dealing with these contaminating 'negativity viruses'?

Try this!

- Be mindful of the kinds of conversations that fill your home, and be bold enough to edit guests who might be building up to a 'complaints and disasters' monologue.

- Watch your child's exposure to the media. Even if material isn't age-restricted, sensitive children are often very vulnerable to distressing imagery.

- At the same time, no matter how careful you are, your child is going to be exposed to some horrible truths about her world. Newspapers, magazines, TV and schoolmates are all efficient carriers of distressing knowledge. If she does encounter something that's troubling her, take the time to

---

hear her thoughts and feelings. Make sure that she has an age-appropriate grasp of what happened. When I talk to a perplexed child, I pay special attention to her thoughts and questions, because these give me an idea of the depth of her understanding and the kind of feedback she needs. By letting her questions guide the conversation, I quickly discover the things that are troubling her and so I know how best to help and reassure her. Stay within the realm of your child's questions and answer these respectfully. You'll find that she is able to use you as a comforting reference point.

- If something is troubling your child, what should she do about it? Is there an age-appropriate response that she can make? Is this the time for her to collect small change from the family to make a donation to charity, help cook a meal or say a prayer?

- Spouses do argue. In fact, research shows that couple arguments do not mean that a marriage is unhealthy (Gottman 2000). But, of course, there are constructive and destructive ways of arguing. Let your children learn the skills of respectful disagreement from you. Let them see how well you listen to each other, how you are able to come to effective compromises and, of course, how you're able to go through the process of apology and forgiveness when one of you has 'blown it'.

- Your child doesn't need you to be emotionally bullet-proof. If you are going through a difficult time, keep relating to him. Consider letting him know a bit about the challenges you are facing, how you are feeling and what you plan to do to make things better. Let him know what he can do to help you. Sometimes this can be as simple as "Please keep making an effort at school". A child benefits from having a clear purpose when there is strain at home.

- Own your fears. If you are inclined to be something of a 'worry pot' then, instead of allowing your fears to spill over into your child, admit this foible to your child. Help her to see that she doesn't necessarily need to feel the things that you feel.

"Shoo! Your first day at high school! I feel quite nervous for you. But then again, you know that I sometimes get silly that way."

Gratitude

The fact that our children overhear our everyday conversations also presents us with some wonderful opportunities. Imagine your child's experience as he overhears your stories of appreciation and excitement. Imagine him overhearing conversations about your successes and triumphs at work: how you finally buttoned down the big deal, or about the glowing compliment you got from a client. How often do we talk about some of the country's successes? How often do we talk about the many things we have to be thankful for?

Studies have linked gratitude to feelings of contentment (Walker & Pitts, 1998), happiness, pride, and hope (Overwalle, Mervielde, & De Schuyter, 1995). In a fairly recent Gallup (1998) survey of American teens, over 90% said that expressing gratitude helped them to feel happy. Emmons and Crumpler (2000) have found that a conscious focus on gratitude makes life more fulfilling, meaningful, and productive. Gratitude connects us to others; it buffers us against envy and helps us to participate in the bigger picture. Gratitude helps us to digest disappointments and setbacks and to enjoy our successes more completely (Emmons & Shelton, 2002).

In my experience, sensitive children who have developed a sense of gratitude are easier to help. They are better able to take ownership of their difficulties and they are more co-operative with their parents. They seem to like themselves more.

Try this!

- I think that sensitive children are able to absorb the orientation of gratitude through simple, everyday interactions with their parents. Whether you're driving in the car, or tucking your child into bed, look out for opportunities to exhibit thankfulness.

- No doubt it's a good idea to teach our children the habit of saying 'thank-you' in their early years. But bear in mind that children probably only start to understand the principles of gratitude by about the age of nine (Gleason & Weintraub, 1976). So, with younger sensitive children, gradually raise their awareness with large dollops of fondness and flexibility.

- As your children get older, let them understand that saying 'thank-you' is not simply about etiquette. It's a way of recognising that they are loved, and that they are able to love.

- Notice acts of kindness in your child and thank him for these deeds.

- Practice showing gratitude in your own life. Many people have found that this works best when it's set in place as part of their daily routines. Consider writing down the things for which you are grateful.

- Gratitude tends to be about 'taking stock'. So don't expect your sensitive child to count her blessings when she's right in the middle of an upset. This kind of emotional whiplash will either leave your child feeling horribly guilty or she'll bite your head off! Wait for calmer waters before reminding your child to reflect on some of the wonderful truths in her life.

- Incorporate gratitude into some of your family rituals (e.g. a word of thanks or prayer before meals, or giving each person the chance to express appreciation for something at the end of every week).

- Teach your children to see the invisible. Encourage them to acknowledge aspects of themselves or their worlds that they routinely overlook.

- Keep your word! Knowing what you are going to do, and when, often makes a big difference to sensitive children. Any underlying hurt, frustration or mistrust will diminish your ability to talk to your child about gratitude.

- In age and ability-appropriate ways, give your children opportunities to help you, and thank them for their efforts.

"Gratitude underlies the appreciation of goodness in others and in oneself."

– Melanie Klein –

Chapter 9

Discipline and the sensitive child

Values based discipline helps family members to see each other better

Parents are normally all too aware of how easy it is to hurt their sensitive child's feelings; that it's often better to overlook the 'small stuff', than to provoke a distressing emotional show-down. At the same time, parents also know that they have to raise their children; that their children need to learn how to become competent, co-operative adults. How do we get the balance right? Here are some thoughts:

Your Child is Wonderful

We must go back to this. I really don't think that it is possible to discipline well without an abiding realisation that your child is deep-down wonderful. Even in loving homes, our efforts to correct our child will go sour if we let this knowledge slip. By this I mean that we harbour misgivings; that there's something fundamental about our child's personhood that we think really needs to change in order for him to be OK.

Beyond their awareness, many good parents discipline in harmful ways because they are reacting from a place of unacknowledged doubt or disappointment. This is when we lash out, either physically or verbally. We criticise, compare, or belittle; or we shake, shove or otherwise hurt our child. Yet none of this means that there is an absence of love!

In 2003, a group of New Zealand researchers tracked the development of 1000 children and found that the children's observed personalities at age the age of three were very similar to their reported personality traits at the age of twenty-six (Caspi, et. al, 2003). In a very real sense, children are who they are.

Children of Conscience

Sensitive children tend to have a keen sense of fairness; of right and wrong. Along with this, many are also very prone to acute experiences of shame when they feel that they have done something wrong (e.g. "I'm useless! Why do I keep doing everything wrong!"). Now shame is not an altogether bad emotion, as it keeps us aware of others and from letting ourselves down. Feeling ashamed of our actions or choices can be the first step towards good behaviour. But this is very different from being ashamed of who we *are*. If we scold our sensitive children when they express their inner natures; their fears, hesitancies, or personal preferences, our children will be ashamed of who they are. How does a child recover from that without withdrawing from, or opposing his parent?

"If it's worth doing, it's worth doing well" was my father's mantra when we were growing up. I hadn't realised how much I've taken that view on board, until my son and I started having nightly battles over his homework. He just doesn't seem to care the way I think he should and it drives me up the wall! I know that I can get quite nasty about it. I felt terrible after I tore his project up and forced him to start over. He started to cry but I just got angrier. I yelled at him, telling him to grow up and stop being so useless. I lost it! I've started to dread homework times and I know he has too.

On the other hand, when a child knows that you know he is wonderful, shame can mobilise him towards positive behaviour. He knows that a burst of naughtiness in no way defines him, that he may have let himself down for a moment, but that both of you know that his more authentic, loveable self is ready and waiting in the wings. Your child has a constant 'best self': an internal resource that allows for healthy responses such as remorse, apology, forgiveness and reconciliation.

"Marjorie, I can't believe that you spoke to me so badly this morning! It just isn't you! You know I'm excited for you, but helping you with your dress is the very last thing I want to do right now. I won't be spoken to that way."

Assessing our levels of faith can be challenging. A breakdown in faith is often subtle, requiring that we take some time to reflect and perhaps talk with our partners. If there's a part of your child's nature that riles you, that you don't trust, this could affect the integrity of your interactions with your child. I believe that we have to check ourselves periodically. All children go through phases when they can be difficult to like. But, when all is said and done, do we maintain an implicit faith in our child, and do we convey this to him?

Think Values

Recognising that our children are great does not mean that 'anything goes'. Far from it! We have to teach our children how to be good to others, and to manage themselves with wisdom. And so we point them towards universally recognised *core values* such as honesty, fairness, respect, responsibility and compassion (Kidder, 2005; Prozesky, 2007). In due course, we have to get grumpy with our children when they ignore our needs. And we have to let them know when we think they have let themselves down through lack of effort, or self respect. We must call our children to join us in the challenge of living ethical lives.

Taking the time to do this makes sense because:

- Practicing good values is vital if our children are to have healthy relationships and productive lives. You can only get so far in life if you think that courtesy is a sign of weakness, or that reward comes without effort.

- Relationships flourish when a family commits to living out good values. Everyone has to be in it together. If family life has gone grotty, it will be because one or more core values are being flouted. Good values are implicitly relational. Respect and honesty are two-way practices (a child can't be honest with a parent who isn't honest with himself). One-sided responsibility can only last so long. Parents open themselves to their children's scrutiny: they must 'walk the talk'. But this is balanced by the emerging, value-based expectations that we must have of our children. As they mature, we must expect our children to relate to us with honesty, compassion, responsibility and respect.

- Sometimes we take issue with our children because of personal assumptions and prejudices rather than stand-alone values. For example, I know that I'm often more patient with my children when they're doing something that I like. However, if they're behind a computer, I'm curt and perhaps even dismissive as I call them to the dinner table. Fair enough, you may say. But if I'm not clear on the values driving my behaviour, and if I'm not able to inspire these within my children, then they are likely to feel personal shame and perhaps resentment as they move towards the dinner table. It happens so easily! They may experience guilt, but if their only recourse is to disown something that they genuinely like to get my favour, they will not have grown as ethical beings.

- When our disciplinary choices are consciously aligned with good values, they will have a reassuring common sense about them. Sensitive children understand values. They know that we should draw the line when someone in the family is being dishonest or thoughtless. In fact, our children need us to enforce these principles. People get hurt when good values are ignored.

- As I've just indicated, many sensitive children have an intuitive grasp of good values, or ethics. Because of this, rules based on good values will reassure sensitive children, and they are likely to be good at contributing to their practice.

- Helping our children to live according to good values gives them something to aim at, and boosts their sense of identity (e.g. *"Mom says that I am a kind/ helpful/responsible/honest person"*)

Deciding to make the link between our rules and values more overt means that we need to know what we stand for and why. But we should also let our growing children to bump up against us from their own perspectives. We need to be prepared to listen and be open to the fact that our children will teach us. Ethical living happens through dialogue.

> *Just recently I've started to challenge my sensitive son on his table manners-something I've pretty much ignored through his younger years. It just seems that, now that he's into the teenage years, he really should start to cut his potato (in half at least!) rather than doing the whole python thing. I've tried not to go on at him about it - I know he gets upset. But the other night he got tearful anyway. He asked me why I was fussing, why now, what about his siblings, and **why** do table manners matter? Well, I know that table manners are important to me. I just need to remember why.*

When families endeavour to behave ethically, parents are less likely to blindly enforce a bunch of hand-me-down rules, and children are less likely to overlook the needs of others. Values-based discipline helps family members to see each other better.

Calm it down

Because of their soft hearted natures, many sensitive children get very agitated or upset when adults get angry with them, often out of proportion to the situation at hand. This doesn't mean that we can't be angry; but it does mean that we should strive to contain our outrage. A sensitive child just becomes too aroused to respond to an approach that is dominated by harsh confrontation, yelling or smacking. He may see your mouth moving, but your words will bounce off the dome of his agitation. Because of the emotional overload, your child will either be flooded by hurt and withdraw from you, or you'll find yourself locked in a 'power struggle'. Both of you will be left feeling horrible inside.

Remember, sensitive children are easily shamed, so keep a light touch. In fact, haranguing a sensitive child by saying things like *"Why did you do that? Tell me you're sorry! What have you learnt"* is not only unnecessary; it is often counterproductive. The child may be so consumed by shame, and feel so exposed, that he has to shift into defence-mode.

Keeping your composure enables you to stay in touch with your child's perspective. He will have one! Without acknowledging this, it's possible that all your sensitive child will be able to 'hear' will be his unmet need; that 'unfair' circumstance which set him off in the first place.

Remember that some sensitive children really struggle to back down from a confrontation. Again, you don't need to become an impassive robot. You are allowed your emotions. I think that the following example would be just as effective if it were said through gritted teeth:

> *"I can see that you're upset; and that your brother can be a pain, but you know that you must come to me before you decide to hit him. Now I am angry with you too."*

Once you have worked to recognise your child's point of view, he will be more able to *calm down*. When we are awash with intense feelings, it's very difficult to listen, or to use our reason. In a range of ways, get your child to understand that he first needs to calm himself before the knot can really be untied. Perhaps you all need to sit down, and not say anything for a while. Just give yourselves a few precious moments to breathe and think. Use your discretion to decide when to reconvene. For most fall-outs, we're talking a few minutes; but family life can get complicated, and sometimes we need to give ourselves a whole day of reflection before we are able to decide how to deal with a problem.

Here's an example of a simple stop, think, and reconvene sequence with a younger child:

Gregory, you are not thinking at the moment and you are act-
ing silly. I need you to stop and come and sit here ... OK, now
I need you to go and say sorry to your sister and then we can
carry on with the game."

Save the teaching for later

Don't try to teach your child, or do a whole lot of explaining, in the heat of the moment. If you do, it's highly likely that your sensitive child will stay upset and defensive. Rash things may be said and little learning will take place. If you think that a situation needs to be talked through, wait until later in the day, when the emotional heat has dissipated. You'll know that your timing is right when, even if your child gets a few tears in his eyes, he's able to have a *conversation* with you about the earlier incident. Both of you are open, able to voice your opinions and listen to other's points of view. It's a time of connection, resolution and healing.

Think Consequences

Our world is sustained by a lattice-work of consequences, good and bad. Sooner or later, we reap what we sow. It is important to let our sensitive children know that they are part of this action-reaction world.

For this reason, I find it helpful to distinguish between *consequences* and *punishments*. As a form of consequence, punishment has its place. But we have to be careful not to set ourselves up as the *authors* of right and wrong. If our discipline is dominated by intimidating punishments, it's all too easy to veer off into ditches of power struggles and resentment, where our children live with the idea that we stand between them and their desires. The values behind our family rules will be obscured if not forgotten. Instead, ways of avoiding punishment will occupy our child's attention. He may comply, but over time he's probably going to find many ways, passive or active, to defy you.

Perhaps it is better for us to see ourselves as *custodians* of right and wrong. We have to show our children how to follow what is good, and when they blow it, we have to let them bump up against the kinds of natural, safe consequences that family life can provide. This prepares our children for a far less forgiving world. It's a daunting responsibility!

Consequences are not about us and how angry or intimidating we can be. Unlike punishments, they don't have to be all that nasty to be effective. The best consequences are often low-key and matter of fact. But they have a natural, value-based logic to them. They are inevitable.

> *"I was watching TV one rainy evening when Dad walked in. He'd noticed that I'd left my brother's cricket bat out on the lawn and he asked me to go and get it. When I started to whine dad simply shrugged his shoulders and said 'Fine; that can be your bat. We'll get your brother a new one instead of the one you were going to get for your birthday.' Well, I bolted out there and fetched that bat. I've never forgotten that evening."*

I think that the best way to leverage a child's behaviour is to work with the rewards and consequences that already exist within the flow of normal life. From this perspective, watching TV, using the computer or getting a lift to visit a friend can all be placed on the other side of co-operative behaviour. So, instead of coming home from school and immediately switching the computer on, a child might understand that this can only happen once his dirty clothes are in the wash basket. And the child understands that, after a time of rest and relaxation, he can only get to watch his favourite evening programme once his homework has been done. If we don't work towards this natural kind of give-and-take, our children are going to believe that the above pleasures are rights. And we'll be left scratching our heads as we try to come up with an escalating list of suitably desirable, exotic rewards (such as gifts).

The list below describes different aspects of 'good consequences'. It's perhaps difficult to meet every aspect all the time, but these guidelines do give us something to aim for.

When it comes to sensitive children, I believe that it's most important that consequences are:

- predictable (children know how the system works)
- short-lived (children can redeem themselves quickly)
- calming (the consequence reduces, rather than raises arousal)

Effective consequences also tend to be:

- structured (part of routine family life, rather than haphazard, 'make it up as you go along' reactions to bad behaviour)
- meaningful (children understand the reasons behind the system)
- valued (children recognise the benefits and costs of their behaviour)
- reasonable (children agree that the system is fair)
- related (there is a clear link between children's behaviour and the costs and benefits)
- immediate (benefits and costs follow shortly after behaviour)

Wherever possible, try to ensure that the costs of bad behaviour are dry and boring whilst the benefits of good behaviour are gratifying and fulfilling. Unfortunately, as many parents can testify, we're inclined to give our energy to the things that we *don't* like in our children. On any given school morning, it's usually the ways that our children aren't co-operating that we zap. On the other hand, when our often dozy, dependent, or wilful children are behaving in a way that actually helps, we're often so relieved that it's hard not to use that time as a welcome opportunity to turn to our own agendas. Whilst this is quite understandable, it does mean that our responses to instances of good behaviour by our children (e.g. responsibility, emotional control, tolerance) may be fairly *neutral*. As these fleeting moments pass, our children are left largely unaware of, and uninspired by, the positive value of their recent actions. How does your child benefit from the many times that he's actually quite likeable? Is he aware of these benefits, and does he value them? Is he proud of the times that he is good?

Remember that the loving relationship you share with your child is your greatest source of influence. Even if he won't admit it, hurting you or 'turning you off' is usually enough of a consequence for a sensitive child. For this reason, many parents of sensitive children have found that additional consequences are unnecessary. Their child is upset and remorseful enough already. However, in some cases, parents can be so protective of their sensitive child that they never let on when they are hurt, offended or upset. If this applies to you, look for appropriate opportunities to let your growing child know when he has upset you, and give him practical ways to reciprocate your care. In this way you prepare him for healthy adult relationships.

"Good parenting requires ... 'mutuality'– a relationship in which not only is the parent attuned to her child's needs but also the child is expected to have some empathic regard for his parent."

– Taffel and Blau –

Have Patience

At any opportunity and over anything you care to think of, our two kids would get into a scrap. Driving in the car with them could drive you to drink: who saw the cow first, who got to choose the music, and who breathed on whom. I used to get most frustrated with my eldest. Surely he was old enough to rise above all the nonsense? But when I had a go at him, he would get very upset, and say that I was being unfair. I had to realise that he just wasn't ready; that who gets to sit in which chair still really mattered to him. Accepting this helped me to lighten up. I clearly remember the one night where the four of us started to list and laugh about all the things that Devon and Michelle had managed to fight over. Although this never actually stopped the squabbles, somehow we moved past them more easily after this.

Someone wise once said that it takes a long time to see how our children will turn out. Many sensitive children are mature in certain respects, and rather immature in others. If you and your sensitive child are continually butting heads over a particular issue, consider whether he is really ready and able to meet your expectations. When we step back and take the long-term view, we are able to be more patient, flexible and creative. Using dimensions such as humour, we are able to move more fluidly past historical sticking points. We preserve the relationship without dropping our principles.

There is only so much that we can control. We can love our children, we can speak and listen to them, and we can ensure that their environment carries reasonable consequences, both good and bad. But that's it! Beyond this, we have no actual control. Our children must unfold in their own ways.

This can be scary. When something is really important to us, we don't want to leave it to chance. Consequently, many of us hold onto one or two favourite ways that we try to control those we love. Perhaps it's that we go silent, and use 'dark looks'. Or perhaps we get big, loud and intimidating. Some of us will swear by the dripping tap technique, with extra pleading or guilt-barbs thrown in where necessary. And who hasn't been thrilled by the chance to retaliate?

> *"You want me to take you where? Well then, you should've listened to me when I asked you to … That'll teach you, heh, heh!"*

However, sooner or later, our carefully arranged controls will fall apart. Our children have to develop their ability to make good choices. Along the way, they will make bad choices. The key question is: to whom will they turn? I want that person to be you.

"Conscience matures slowly,
that is why parents don't favour it."

– S. Soloveychik –

Chapter 10
Children in the grip of worry

Helpful worry keeps us safe,
but unhelpful worry keeps us stuck

Many sensitive children battle with worry (Kagan, 2004). Just about everyone knows what it means to worry. For some of us, however, it's a frequent, destabilising feeling that just won't go away that easily. In fact, some of my clients have had to change their idea of progress, from 'worry free' to 'worry well'. Their goal has become to learn more about their worry, and to understand how best to get on with life despite the effects of this unwelcome presence. New learning often takes place when children discover that there are things that they can do deliberately even though worry has them in a painful grip. These things are often small, perhaps no more than taking a deeper breath. However, these deliberate actions can often be the thin edge of a wedge that can free a child over the years.

Managing worry

Clever lies

Feeling afraid or worried is healthy and normal, but let your child see the difference between helpful and unhelpful worry. Help your child understand that helpful worry keeps us safe, but unhelpful worry keeps us stuck. Because I often talk about worry as a person (Mr Worry) or creature (the Worry Bug), I usually end up talking about the ways that worry tricks us with what I call 'clever lies'. I explain that a clever lie always contains a grain of truth surrounded by a lot of fibs. It's the grain of truth that allows the lie to get into children's heads, but once it's inside, it's the fibs that end up hurting them. And so, for example, I can talk with Michael about the fact that parents do sometimes forget to fetch their children after school. And this is a scary thought! But then we can remember that Michael's mother has never forgotten him, and that Mrs Jenkins always stays at school until all the children have been fetched. These true facts help Michael to deflect worry's clever, terrifying lies about being abandoned.

Helpful and unhelpful worry

Remember, unhelpful worry can feel just as painful and upsetting as helpful worry. The aim is to divert your child away from, rather than to trivialise 'unhelpful' exaggerated worry. Help her to see that unhelpful worry is often caused by what we are thinking or imagining, rather than by some real outside danger. You could ask your child to imagine a time that she usually finds stressful (e.g. waiting to be fetched after sport). Now ask her to imagine how she normally feels. And then, what might she be thinking to make her feel that way? Given time and some suggestions, your child will probably be able to come up with some worried thoughts (e.g. "Mom has forgotten me"). You can show how these thoughts feed her nasty feelings. The situation doesn't carry any real danger, it's the thoughts and pictures or images that come into her mind that are upsetting.

Sensible thinking

You could then ask her to come up with some other thoughts that would help her to step away from unhelpful worry (such as "Mom has been late before but she's never forgotten me", or "Mrs Jenkins won't leave before I do, and she has my Mom's number"). As you and your child seek out more balanced or helpful thoughts, be on the lookout for *realistic* rather than *false* positive thoughts. Remember, worry specialises in clever lies. We might all like to think that nothing bad can happen to the people we love but your child is too smart to be convinced by something that we all know just isn't so.

Some children like to imagine what one of their respected, capable friends would be thinking and doing in a similar situation. How would Nick manage the fact that his Mom is late? How would he pass the time? What would Nick be thinking about?

You want to get to the stage where your child understands 'sensible thinking' well enough to practise it on her own. So when your child is worried, you can then say something like, "Why don't you use your 'sensible' thinking? Let me know what you think of." This means that your child is learning how to use realistic thinking.

What If?

Many sensitive children carry 'what if' worries: 'what if there's an accident', 'what if you forget me', 'what if there's a storm'. because these 'what if's' are so unlikely, many parents instinctively respond by explaining why there's really nothing to fear. Generally speaking, children aren't convinced! They just go quiet. It's often more effective to *follow* your child's thinking: what *could* or *should* she do if this terrible thing ever happened? Help her to construct an action plan. Help your child to build this important habit: when she's worried, what should she *do*?

Parallel Truths

It's really important that we don't dismiss worried thoughts as silly. They have a powerful emotional logic that's not easily denied. Remember, however misguided, worry is based on our primal need to protect ourselves. Respect the emotion. Disagreeing with your child about the surface logic of his worry ("Why are you so worried?") tangles you in an argument that goes nowhere. It's also futile to try and reassure your child that she shouldn't feel worried. It's not just that reassurance doesn't work, it also prevents her from exercising her ability to capture, express and contain her feelings.

Anxious children sometimes have the idea that I want them to *stop* thinking about something that's upsetting them (such as tomorrow's History test). Of course, this never works. Have you ever tried to *not* think about something? Don't you just end up thinking about it even more? Help your child to bypass these potential 'thought wars' by reminding him that we want him to practise thinking about things that he can *also* think about, even though he is worried (e.g. "What happened the last time I wrote a History test?" "What sections do I need to study tonight?").

I also like the idea of writing worries down on scraps of paper and storing them in a 'God box'. Worry is often about control and this activity gives your child a concrete reminder that he can let go and trust in something much bigger than himself. In addition to this, some children and teens might select and write down a list of encouraging, affirming statements. Others might prefer to choose some inspiring pictures. Your child can cut these out and place them in a jar next to the worry box. As your child puts away her worries, she can take out a note or picture that reminds her of some of her healthier truths.

Use the table below to capture some of the thinking behind your child's worries:

Catching Clever Lies
1. My child's worry: (e.g. tomorrow's history test) ....
2. Scary truth (e.g. I might not get the mark I hope for) ....
3. Silly lies (e.g. I will get into serious trouble; if I don't do well, I'm worthless)   ....
4. Reassuring truths (e.g. You don't get punished, even if you fail; I know this work; I can study hard tonight, people like me for who I am)   ....

Practise

Once you and your child have found some healthy self statements (e.g. "I will focus on one sum at a time.") encourage her to practise using them when she's actually feeling distressed. If we want new ways of thinking to be effective, we need to practise them in real life. Early on, I encourage children to practise saying the statements to me or to their parents. Then, when they're familiar with the words, I ask them to practise saying the phrases under their breath when they're in a stressful situation. This seems to help them to pay attention to the reassuring thought. Some children also like to write their helpful thoughts down on cards so that they can read them whenever anxiety starts to squeeze.

Keeping busy

Many children have told me that 'keeping busy' really helps them when they feel nervous. Where possible, you and your child can think of some absorbing or distracting activities that he can turn to, while turning his back on worry.

Possible distractions:

- Reading
- Helping around the home
- Engaging in a hobby
- Phoning a friend/family member
- Visiting a friend/family member
- Exercise/going for a walk
- Playing with a sibling
- Playing with a pet

For younger children

'Thinking about our thinking' is a fairly abstract, mature skill. So, if your child is under the age of 7, don't be surprised if the most she gives you is a vague, distracted smile as you start to talk about worried thoughts. Perhaps she just isn't ready to think about herself in this way. All children can do with a comforting hug when they're distressed, but younger children, especially, will really need us to step in and physically soothe them. As we do this, we can still raise their awareness of available parallel truths. And then we can help them to busy themselves with that distraction.

"Ooh yes, she is quite a big dog! (You calmly pick your young child up) *Shame sweetheart, did you get a fright?* (You hug and cuddle your child) *Look how she's wagging her tail ... Just let me pet her for a little bit.* (You stand still for a moment, giving some time for your child's arousal to drop) *And she's got lovely, thick fur. Can you feel her fur with your feet?* (If your child is starting to respond, you continue to stay there for a moment or two) *Oh look there's Michelle at the swings, let's go and say 'Hi'* (You walk off, with your child perhaps still in your arms)."

In all of this, the substance of your message doesn't lie in your words. It's your non-verbal mix of compassion, comfort, and calm authority that 'speaks' to your child.

Rating worry

Worry is not a constant experience: it tends to ebb and flow, especially when we are prepared to confront it. Many children have found that it's helpful to rate how strong their worry feels at any given time. I usually ask younger children to tell me how 'high' their worry is (a metre off the floor, halfway to the ceiling, or close to the top). When children are a bit older, I use analogies like 'rev' counters or thermometers to get a sense of how intense the worry feels.

Plan and predict

Studies show that sensitive children are often thrown by unexpected challenges. If you think this applies to your child, then teach her to think through upcoming events and to plan and predict as much as possible. Help her to forecast likely scenarios, and to come up with a range of possible responses that she can make. Many older children have found this helpful when it comes to things like impending school trips or competitions. In a similar vein, many sensitive children don't like surprises. Where possible, tell your child about upcoming events so that she can feel more emotionally prepared.

Or Not!

Then again, some parents have found that it's sometimes better *not* to give their sensitive child too much time to think. Rather, before she knows it she's bundled into the car and, as you look in the rearview mirror, you're thrilled to see that she's laughing along with her friends. Perhaps different situations call for different approaches, and we need to use our discretion to decide whether our children will benefit from advanced warning or not.

Change the focus

When worry bites, it tends to absorb our focus. Show your older child how she can deliberately change her focus of attention. Perhaps you could start by asking her to describe the sensations in her body. Can she feel her heart beating? Help her to describe her breathing? How do her muscles feel? Now help her to change her focus to things outside her body. Is the day warm or hot? What can she see, smell and hear? Then she can shift her attention back to her inner self again. This simple exercise shows your child that she has some control over the things that occupy her mind at any given moment. She can learn some critical micro-skills that will help her to notice her feelings in finer detail, without being swamped by them.

To help younger children with the same the idea, I sometimes have fun with them by suggesting and imagining silly images, like a purple pig or a Giraffe with dreadlocks. Children can also deliberately remember a happy event, or think about something that they are looking forward to. They can also use favourite photographs to prompt their imaginations.

....

I've sometimes thought that managing worry is a bit like trying to land a fighter jet on an aircraft carrier. The engine is revving, the target is small and slippery and the seas are high and dark. For anxious children to learn how to find their landing zone, they need to be guided by parents who give calm and clear directions and who are confident enough to hold the landing beacons still. Also, as any flight controller will tell you, parents are allowed to adjust the tone of their instructions to suit the situation. It can sometimes help to be really firm and direct with a child who's in the process of 'losing it'.

Through our attitudes, actions and words, we need to teach our sensitive children not to be afraid of being afraid, because that kind of emotional stance brings no lasting relief. Instead, we need to gradually show our worried children how to accept, understand and work *with* their worries.

"The one-word antidote for all anxiety problems is acceptance."

– Du Pont Spencer et. al. –

Chapter 11

Doing things that make us tougher

Become brave by being brave

Aristotle suggested that we become brave by doing brave acts. Many successful people will tell you that repeatedly doing something daunting can melt the edges off fear. By contrast, the more we avoid something, the more our fears can harden. Avoidance feeds fear. Your child needs to understand that there is a limit to how frightened he can be, and that choosing to push towards this plateau gives him a chance first to tolerate, and then to rise above his fears. As a child is guided through this lesson, he meets, perhaps for the time, his innate courage.

Learning to face one's fears and worries is a significant challenge for anyone. It can be very difficult to stand by and allow your child to go through a tunnel of worry. Here are some thoughts that might help you to form your own stance on the matter:

Pick your battles

Help your child to tackle things that he feels ready to. If you've high-lighted some encouraging exceptions in your child's behaviour (see Chapter 7), then you can work with the momentum that these real-life examples give to him.

Allow your child to set the pace

Children, and perhaps teenagers in particular, are likely to have quite strong opinions regarding what they will and won't confront and how they want to do this. I find that it is better to allow your child to set the pace as much as possible, especially if she is anxious about many areas of her life. If you don't respect this, your child will end up re-sisting your efforts. Remember, your goal is to get your child used to what it feels like to stare down her anxiety. It really doesn't matter which challenge she chooses.

Choose practical goals

It's much easier if you pick goals that you can practise and monitor. Let me confess that I've found 'sleep problems' tough to change for this very reason. Whether it's a child who doesn't want to sleep in his own bed, or doesn't want to stay over at friends' houses, it's hard to help a child to confront this problem. Sleep is a passive activity that's tough to do deliberately. And then, it's not easy to come up with step-by-step approaches to 'sleep-outs'. I've tended to find that this particular problem is best solved when a child is mature enough to want to challenge herself. She then sets up, and controls the gradual learning that is necessary. The alternative would be for you to make a tough, executive decision and insist that she get back into routine and healthy sleeping habits. This is not always easy to do and it's likely to mean a few sleepless nights for you. Perhaps it's worth it. Remember though, that it's very unlikely that your child will want to sleep in the same room as you after his eighteenth birthday. But don't phone me if he does!

Seriously though, if everyone is getting enough sleep in the home, and your child continues to grow in other areas of his life, consider tolerating mix and match sleep arrangements until your child is ready for more independent routines (over the age of 7 perhaps?). If you do decide that 'enough is enough' and that your child is old enough to move towards greater independence, consider the suggestions included in the appendix section at the end of the book.

Break the challenge down

Once your child has chosen a challenge (e.g. participating more in class), break it down into a sequence of small and concrete steps (e.g. start by agreeing to go up to the teacher's desk to ask a question once a day, during Maths). If she is able to repeat the early goal often, she should feel a sense of growth and be able to tackle a slightly bigger goal if necessary. This can take a bit of time, and some days will go better than others. Be patient!

Work together

It really helps if you and your partner are 'on the same page' when it comes to supporting your child as he confronts a fear. It's very easy for things to fall apart if he senses that his parents don't agree on the process.

Reward success

Celebrate your child's progress, and reward her efforts. Praise can't be underestimated but concrete rewards also go a long way (a favourite meal or chocolate and congratulatory note on your child's pillow?)

Try to make the rewards immediate and accessible. Very few children will stay motivated when the reward lies a month away.

Some parents have told me that they don't like using rewards because it feels like they are bribing their children. My response to that is that good and bad consequences are an integral part of the way the world works. Just about everything we do is intentional and is based on perceived benefits. This includes intangible benefits like satisfaction, or a sense of achievement. It's not just about buying presents for our children. How many of us would choose to work without some kind of reward (material or non-material)? For me, bribery involves utilising natural leverage for wrongful purposes. It's not the leverage that is wrong.

Practise scenarios

If you're willing, act out the challenge with your younger child so that he's had a few practise runs before the real event. For example, where the fear is linked to the classroom, you could have fun being the teacher as your child practises being brave, and then swap round!

With a younger child, consider making up a bed time story that somehow relates to the challenge that she faces. It sometimes helps to use characters that your child knows (fictional or otherwise) and don't think the story has to be particularly good or clever. Even if you'd really blush if someone overheard your attempt, remember that something special always happens when a parent takes the time to tell a story to a child.

Knowing the feeling

Remember that 90% of anxiety's power hits *before* we attempt something daunting and so we have to know what it feels like to summon ourselves and press forwards *despite* the worry. This 'pressing forwards feeling' is what you want your sensitive child to know, not just in his head but in his body. Where necessary, you need to use your ingenuity and encouragement to help him to experience this truth. He has to know what if feels like to go *over* the mountain, and that he *will* feel better if only he doesn't turn back too soon. Whether it's going out to play sport, make a speech, or write a test, I like to use examples from children's own lives to illustrate the point that they can be brave, and that we almost always feel better once we've actually started something.

Reminding your child of other times that he has been brave helps him to know that, at an emotional level, he's been down this road before. He's calling on an ability that is already inside him. Take a moment to list some of the times that your child has tolerated fear or worry. However small, they are important early markers of your child's emotional strength.

My child was brave when he/she:
1. ....
....
2. ....
....
3. ....
....
4. ....
....

When a child has been brave, I often take the opportunity to discuss the experience with her. I ask her what the most difficult part of doing something scary was, how she managed to do it and how she felt afterwards. I listen out for the words that she uses so that we can start to build up a private, personal vocabulary for her experience of 'facing fear'. When another challenge comes along, I use this vocabulary again, because then the child quickly understands what we're talking about.

Also, when children have made some progress with their worries, I make an effort to capture and reinforce the learning. When calm and confident, children are able to see that facing fear is an important part of overcoming fear. But during anxious times, children tend to forget. It's quite common for anxious children to experience set backs, and I just know that they won't want to believe an old truth when they're experiencing new fears. So, shortly after some success, take a bit of time to really review the triumph with your child. Can she come up with a catch-phrase (e.g. 'keeping busy really helps me') to describe her recent experience?

....

The following story shows what some of these suggestions (including Chapter 10) might look like in real life:

	STRATEGIES
I think it's fair to say that Cameron has always been sensitive. He just gets thrown by the silliest things. He still hasn't plucked up the nerve to spend nights with friends and I really don't know what we're going to do when school trips come his way. He works hard and he's usually happy to go to school, thank goodness! But this year started really badly. For the first time he has a male teacher and he started to get so stressed about getting into trouble. He has never liked to get things wrong. I got worried when he started to say that he didn't want to go to school in the mornings.	Sensitive children can be thrown by new things
	Impulse to avoid
Although he has a loud voice, his teacher is actually a really nice guy and we decided to chat to him about the situation. He'd said that Cameron was withdrawn and passive in the classroom and that he seemed to prefer to 'fly below the radar'. We wanted to use this situation as an opportunity for Cameron to stretch himself a bit.	Where appropriate, work with the teacher
The next day I spoke with Cameron about how worry seemed to be giving him a hard time at school, especially when it came to Mr Jones. I asked him what worry was making him feel, where he felt these feelings in his body, and when the feelings were worst. Cameron said that he felt 'nervous', especially at the start of the day, and also during Maths, when Mr Jones seemed to 'get all strict'.	Help your child to talk about his/ her feelings. If suitable, use 'externalisation'

He said that most of the horrible feelings were in his tummy and also that he felt like crying in his throat. We noticed how the bad feelings were usually worst at the beginning (of the day and of Maths). We spoke a bit about the difference between helpful worry and unhelpful worry. I said I thought that things were bad at the beginning because Cameron hadn't started to listen to his sensible thoughts yet. We wondered together about what worry might be saying to him to upset him at those times, and, following my lead, Cameron said that worry was telling him that he was going to get into trouble.

Look for specifics, including body tension

Teach anti-worry principles

We then talked about how worry was lying. It made out that Mr Jones is a horrible person and that getting into trouble or getting things wrong is worse than it really is. We spoke about what actually happens when someone makes mistakes, or gets into trouble at school, and about how the teachers never actually hurt any children. Cameron spoke about one of his friends, who has been in detention a couple of times, and that he had been OK about it.

Cameron and I then spoke about ways that he could feel stronger at school. We practised some tummy breaths together and we came up with the words "I am safe here" for Cameron to practise holding in his mind at the start of the day.

Practise skills together. Have fun!

Because he felt better once the school day had started we also thought about how he could 'start sooner' by keeping busy as soon as he went into the classroom. To be honest, he found the 'thought and relaxation' process difficult, but at least he has something that he can keep practising whenever he feels nervous.	Break the challenge down
Mr Jones was such a star! He spoke to Cameron a couple of days later and encouraged him to come up to his desk and chat early on in the day. As Cameron started to do this, Mr Jones told him privately how pleased he was and how well he was doing. Mr Jones also kept us posted by writing comments in Cameron's homework notebook, so my husband and I could praise and encourage him from our side. I think Cameron quite likes his teacher now. The other day I actually heard him encourage his sister when she was grumbling about school.	Move towards the fear Reward success Continue onwards, hopefully a little wiser, towards the next bump in the road

Be patient

Although it's counter-intuitive, we have to get our children used to the feeling of standing firm in the midst of their fears, and acting. Anxious children are going to struggle if they stiffen, panic and look to flee each time worry visits. It's really hard, but our children need to learn how to acknowledge and *step into their fears*, at both a physical (what's happening to me?) and a cognitive (what am I imagining?)

level. This 'flexibility under fire' is a distinct skill, best learnt in incremental ways. When it comes to this particular art, no-one gets a black belt after the first few classes.

Please don't forget that your sensitive child is going to mature past many of her difficulties. And, bear in mind that as she matures, she will be more and more ready to embrace new situations that can bring about surprising bursts of growth.

The important thing about a problem is not it's solution, but the strength we gain in finding a solution.

– Paul Lee Tan –

Chapter 12

Biased brooding

*We do not simply respond to 'the way things are',
we respond to our interpretations of
'the way things are'.*

Many sensitive children go through phases where they feel 'down'. They tend to be a thoughtful bunch, but we need to pay attention to the patterns that these thoughts start to form. A steady stream of worried thoughts can easily lead to pools of negativity, where cycles of self-criticism and hopelessness build.

Sensitive children, particularly those who carry streaks of perfectionism, can be inclined to take setbacks badly. This form of anxiety tends to highlight all the things that aren't right and blocks a child's capacity to enjoy his accomplishments. People are meaning-makers. We do not simply respond to 'the way things are', we respond to *our interpretations* of 'the way things are'. It seems that we tend to become habitual in the ways that we interpret our world.

The importance of optimism

Studies have emphasised the benefits of teaching our children to remain optimistic in the face of setbacks. Children who've learnt the habit of optimism are happier, they tend to do well at school, are more confident and make friends easily (Seligman, 1990; Snyder, 2002). Consider how important optimism is in life. Just about anything worth doing will include frustrations and disappointments. If we don't learn to digest these and keep moving, then fairly soon we won't even be prepared to start a project. The good news is that holding onto an optimistic attitude during the tough times is a skill that can be learned!

Self talk

Start to listen to the ways your child explains the world, particularly as he confronts something that's difficult for him. Does he constantly criticise himself? Is he starting to say gloomy things like "This will never come right"? When he's feeling disappointed, does he behave as though his whole world has fallen apart? These pessimistic habits of thinking place a child at risk for mood difficulties. Seligman (2002) calls these negative habits *personal, permanent,* and *pervasive*: when things go wrong it's because there's something wrong with me (personal); things will never improve (permanent) and my whole life is pretty much ruined (pervasive). Ouch!

If you do notice your child becoming overly negative in any of these ways, it's natural to want to correct and encourage her. But at the same time, don't make the mistake of becoming her life-long optimism depot. Of course you want to encourage your child when she's 'down', but it's also really important to highlight what she's doing *to herself,* so that she can begin to take personal responsibility for correcting her thinking style. Don't spend a lot of energy trying to convince her to think more positively: rather focus your efforts on raising her awareness of *what she's doing to herself.* After acknowledging that she is upset, you may want to encourage *her* to come up with less self-critical, more hopeful responses and solutions and then praise her efforts in this regard.

"Our daughter sets herself high standards, and she gets really down on herself when things don't turn out the way she'd hoped. The other day I was going through her school report with her. I thought it was a really good report, but all she focussed on was the mildly negative comment she got from one of the teachers.

Later on that day I spoke to her about her habit of seeing things as 'half empty' rather than 'half full'. Since that day I just have to say the words 'half empty' and she knows what I'm talking about and what I want her to do."

It's not always easy to know what a child is 'saying' to herself. In fact, as Buzan (2005) reminds us, we tend to think in the language of imagery rather than words. Many of our attitudes and beliefs haven't ever been put into actual words. How then, can we access and influence our child's on-going 'inner counsel'? Let your child's moods guide you. If you notice that she's been feeling low for a while, you can be assured that she is seeing her world from a negative perspective. Knowing this enables you to have the following kind of conversation:

"Sue honey, you've been looking really sad for a while now. What's wrong?"

"You shouted at me."

"Well ... sorry. But what you did really annoyed me ... Sue that was yesterday, why are you still sad? What's going on inside that head of yours?"

From a conversation like this your child can begin to put her thoughts into words, and both of you are now able to 'see' what has, up to now, been invisible. You now have something to work with.

Managing biased brooding

Healthy thoughts

Help your child to come up with some healthy, reassuring thoughts that she can dwell on instead. Help her to see that these are alternative truths that she can use to balance her unrealistic, sad thoughts. I've just said that imagery is a natural language of the brain. I find that children remember healthy thoughts better if they are tied to a recognisable image. Try it for yourself. Generate some positive personal symbols.

> *"Sue, there's nothing that you could do that would change my love for you! I want you to remember what I've just said. Think of the big rock on Granny's farm that you and I like to sit on together to remind you."*

Once your child grasps the idea of 'healthy thoughts', you can begin to ask her to come up with her own versions if she slips into a negative mindset. Remember, though, that healthy thoughts are *realistic*. Children's hearts are not swayed by false assurances. As Reivich and Shatte (2002) say: when you are able to come up with a positive but plausible perspective, "you'll feel it in your gut." (p.211)

Beware of rumination

If your child is really battling to escape a low mood you might notice that he's repeatedly bombarding himself with just a few discouraging thoughts (e.g. I'm not handsome, I have no friends, I'll never pass Matric). This is called *rumination* and it's a truly rotten, destructive habit. It's not always easy to shift a person away from this kind of thinking – it can be a strangely comfortable hole for people to settle into. But at the very least I encourage you to make your child aware of what he's doing to himself. You really want to nip this development in the bud if you can. It can be so destructive that professional advice on ways to interrupt this pattern may well be necessary.

I think that each of us carries a range of beliefs about ourselves and our worlds, some of which are optimistic, and some of which are pessimistic. The ratios may vary from person to person. Some lucky people seem to have been born 'sunny side up'. Still, even the melancholic has a set of keys from which she can choose. We all have access to a particular array of personal truths, some of which are nourishing, some of which are harmful. And these beliefs are a part of who we are. Whenever I talk with children who are battling with low mood, it soon becomes clear that they are dwelling on a surprisingly small corner of themselves. Teach your child to look around, and to be careful about where she decides to settle.

Accept your parental limits

It can be literally gruelling to walk alongside a child who is feeling down or, even worse, depressed. When children are battling in this way I think it's realistic for parents to adjust their expectations and carry their children more. Still, over time real discernment is needed regarding how much responsibility children need to take for their own well-being. Although it may be terrifying, we parents have to accept that there are limits to our influence. As our children get older, they are going to have to take increasing responsibility for their emotional management. Perhaps there are advantages to starting these loving lessons while our children are still young.

Monitor yourself

Be aware of the ways you respond to the frustrations that come your way. When it comes to self-talk, what sort of role model are you? When things are going badly it can feel really gratifying to have a good moan, and none of us wants to be interrupted mid-stream. But how do you counsel yourself after you've had a good rant? Does your child hear and learn from you as you dust yourself off and start to look on the bright side again?

How do you explain your child's failings? What do you say to her when she frustrates you? Make sure that she's not building up a cluster of permanent, personal labels from your moments of irritation (e.g. I'm the clumsy, thoughtless, lazy one).

Be wary of overprotection

It's easy to overprotect a sensitive child, especially if we tend to be 'worry pots' as parents. The thing is, even though the world can be dangerous, children have to know what it feels like to stretch themselves through daring challenges. We grow when we do something daunting, whether it's doing a somersault into the pool, spending the night in a tent or organising a theme party with friends. When we manage to pull something off, we feel more confident about ourselves and our sense of hope grows. We start to accumulate a vital cluster of success memories that we can tap into when the next challenge comes along. So if you feel your anxiety rising whenever your child tries something a little daring, ask yourself whether you are *catastrophising* or not. If you decide that you are, stop, take a deep breath, and ask your partner to make you another cup of tea.

Keep moving

When a child is feeling blue I'll sometimes talk about the way sad thoughts can build a cloud overhead, which blocks out the light and warmth that happier truths could bring. Because of this, I encourage children not to stand still, but to make themselves a 'moving target'. Also, studies tend to show that it's easier to bring about good feelings by *doing* than by *thinking* (Watson, 2000). I want children to have friends, fun and fruitful activities that they can turn to when the clouds are forming.

It's well documented that exercise can be brilliant at breaking up the clouds. I do find though, that I often have to think about the difference between formal, organised recreation and more care-free, unstructured physical expression. Some of the sensitive children I've seen are highly driven, and I don't think that sports practises necessarily offer them much in the way of relief. Sometimes we've had to come up with alternatives that give children a chance to forget and unwind; activities like swimming for fun, or jumping on a trampoline.

....

Perhaps we don't take our thoughts seriously because they seem so abstract and fleeting. But, contrary to the evidence of cartoon strips, our thoughts don't take place somewhere in the air above us. Our thoughts, beliefs and attitudes are in fact very much a part of our physical selves and they have real effects on the way we go about our lives. Remember that intimate neural connections lie behind our thoughts. Each time a brain cell transfers its load of neurotransmitters to another cell (which is a different way of describing a thought), a pathway is blazed that invites repeat transfers. And each time a thought pathway is followed it becomes increasingly habitual and resistant to change. We need to pay careful attention to the beliefs that take shape in our children's minds.

"It is the truth we ourselves speak, rather than the treatment we receive, that heals us."

– O. Hobart Mowrer –

Chapter 13

Growth Channels

*Sensitive children need to learn
how to ride out their emotional waves*

It's difficult and uncomfortable to feel afraid, hurt, frustrated or sad. Many of us will take great care to avoid these feelings. Whole lives are often planned around this apparently simple goal. This is quite understandable. Difficult emotions are, well, difficult. But high-reactive children often experience too many difficult episodes, in too many routine situations, for avoidance to be the only strategy. As parents, we have to think about the ways that we might play a role in this pattern of avoidance. Although it's hard, sensitive children have to learn how to ride out their emotional waves.

Gottman (2004) describes four reactions that parents typically have when their children display negative emotions. Some parents might be *critical* of their children during these times, giving the impression that it's somehow wrong to feel these ways. Other parents might be *dismissive* of their children's expression of difficult emotions, which carries the message that the feelings should be ignored because they are silly or unnecessary. Then there are the parents whom Gottman describes as *laissez-faire* in their approach. These parents are only too happy to sympathise with their children when they are feeling upset but they don't teach them effective ways of responding to the emotions or the situations that cause them. Gottman urges parents to become what he terms *'emotional coaches'*. An emotional coach helps her child to identify and describe her feelings. She also teaches her child a range of healthy responses to these emotions. An emotional coach is sympathetic, but she doesn't expend a lot of energy trying to reassure her child that "everything is going to be ok". She helps her child to look for sensible solutions. She doesn't try to convince him that "there's no need to feel that way", because she knows that horse has already bolted. She knows that it's how we learn to contain our emotions and act that counts.

Some time ago a parent called to tell me about the progress that her sensitive child had made. She described how he had become more 'open', that he had 'learnt how to pace himself, how to manage himself' and that he had realised that he didn't have to simply 'give in' to worry. This is crucial. When our children learn what it feels like to take an *active* stance towards their emotions, they are well on the road towards lifelong resilience.

Let's look again at Kagan's work with high-reactive or inhibited infants. He found that only about one third of these infants carried their timid symptoms into adulthood. This is really encouraging, but notice that change (or growth) occurred because of the ways that most of these youngsters had learned to *respond* to their sensitivity. At a physiological level, these young adults were still emotionally reactive, but they had built up a steady history of healthy responses to their emotional arousal. They had learnt, with growing confidence, how to channel themselves.

Parents play a central role in helping their children to build this emotional history. The early years might require a lot of support and containment, as sensitive children learn more about themselves and the world. When the emotional wobbles come, parents are close by to support, explain and advise. But over the years there is a passing of the baton. Children learn that they are responsible for their emotional lives. They internalise their parents' guidance. Parents remain available as sources of wisdom and encouragement, but it's the children who have to live by the choices they make.

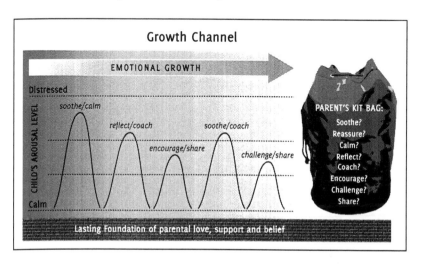

As you can see from the above diagram, I predict that the road ahead is not going to be entirely smooth for your sensitive child. In all probability, there are going to be many, many bumps along the way. Please don't try to flatten every one of them out. As long as your child is learning how to come down once she's gone up, these incidents can be treated as little more than the inevitable speed bumps that we all have to face as we clock up the mileage. You will also notice that the nature and amount of your input should change as your child gets older, from high maintenance, hands on soothing to more adult suggestions and reflections. This is not always the case, as many sensitive children go through one or two particularly challenging emotional patches, perhaps coinciding with puberty, or some other change in their lives. During these times our children will need closer comfort and support. Old emotional lessons may need to be relearned. Nevertheless, despite these (perhaps inevitable) setbacks, I think it's fair to say that a general pattern of emerging emotional independence is something that we should look out for.

Too challenging?

Parents sometimes ask me how to tell whether a period of challenge is going to build or damage their child. It's an important question, because not all challenges are necessarily good for your child. Life can sometimes throw up challenges that children aren't yet equipped to face. Consequently, they get distressed in intense, debilitating ways. So how do we know whether our child is coping with a period of challenge? Well, remember that the critical lesson we want sensitive children to learn is how to *shift* from distress to calm. As Goleman (2004) says: "repeating that sequence of fear-turning-into-calm apparently shapes the neural circuitry for resilience, building an essential emotional capacity." (p.185) It's a fluid, dynamic, and ultimately loving growth process. You must see movement, from distress to calm. So, for instance, if you are told that your child is able to settle into her school day shortly after you leave the classroom, then you can comfort yourself knowing that you're on the right track even though she may be quite tearful when you say goodbye.

However, children can be overwhelmed by stress that is too intense, that goes on too long, or that is too unexpected (Dienstbier & Pytlik Zillig, 2002). You will know that your child is overwhelmed when one or two days pass, and yet she just can't settle her distress. She may be becoming more and more moody, tearful and insecure, or she may be battling with on-going feelings of agitation and fearfulness. The healthy cycle of stress, calm, rest and recover has been broken. Your child is showing you that she can't cope and, as parents, you need to step up your support right away. You also need to think carefully about seeking the guidance and support of relevant mental health professionals.

Work Together

When I was a student, a friend of mine did lifeguard duties to earn some extra cash. Whenever he swam out to assist people in distress, he would carry a flotation device for them to hold onto as they made their way back to shore. I remember him saying that people would sometimes be quite panicked and fatigued. In that state they often clung onto him for all they were worth. My friend described how he would have to get quite tough with them, even to the point of 'bop-ping' his charges on the head with the device if they wouldn't take hold of it and kick. Unless people made some effort to swim for them-selves, both lifeguard and swimmer could end up getting into trouble with the currents.

How do you react when your child gets emotional? Most of us tend to respond in habitual ways. At the risk of over-generalising, I find that moms and dads often react quite differently to their children's emo-tions. Many dads look to suppress or divert their children's emotions whereas moms tend to step in, soothe and solve. Both reactions have their downsides. When fathers habitually block, divert or criticise their children's emotional expression, vital, intimate connections are dam-aged. Trust, spontaneity and emotional warmth are compromised. Mothers who habitually step in to protect their children from emo-tional pain can end up suppressing their children's personal growth. And then, of course, these mothers carry the discomfort of feeling like the 'ham in the sandwich', always on call, always the problem solver. So fathers are perhaps at risk of pushing their sensitive children too hard, or too quickly, whereas mothers may be at risk of allowing their children to continually avoid life's challenges.

When you think about it, a *combination* of these two typical reactions is required. In fact, I often find myself encouraging moms and dads to combine their points of view, especially when there has been disagree-ment about the best way to handle a child's emotional difficulties.

Generally speaking, some combination of love and toughness, or care and confrontation is what's required. I hope that seeing things in this way will help both parents to react more naturally, knowing that their instincts are right. But I also want parents to see the benefits of respecting and making space for their partner's perspective.

Emotional training for Fathers

Author and psychologist Terrence Real (2002) says that, in our culture, boys are typically encouraged to be strong, logical, independent and stoical. In a boys' world, displays of emotion are often targeted and expunged as signs of weakness. With this kind of upbringing, many of us are left quite suspicious of emotions, both in ourselves and in others. We just don't trust the 'touchy-feely' stuff. This can make it hard for us to empathise with and support our sensitive children. I think that many fathers tend to withdraw from their emotional daughters, until their wives have done a suitable 'mop-up' job. And when it comes to our sons, I think that we're inclined to criticise or reject their displays of emotional 'weakness'. I think that we do this, not because we don't love our sons, but because we don't want them to suffer out there in the world. We want to toughen them up.

But if fathers stay stuck in these ways of reacting to their emotional children, everybody loses. In her research, Elaine Aron (2002) found that involved, engaged fathers were especially beneficial to sensitive children, because dads usually play such a key role in introducing their children into the outside world. This kind of support can mean so much to our hesitant children! They need us to help them *with* and not *in spite of* their emotions.

Of course, if we fathers allow some of our male anxieties to dominate then we'll also lose. Our hidebound habits will limit our ability to stay close to our kids just when they need us most and our ability to be a father will be affected. For as long as we ignore or reject our children's emotional experiences, we disrupt intimacy.

Several years ago, on a clear, crisp, Saturday morning, our little family set off for the local pre-primary school. Ahead lay my eldest son's first significant foray into the world of sport; a mini marathon around the school's dinky-sized playground. Unbeknown to me, one of my submerged and cherished fantasies had kicked into gear: at the ripe-and-ready age of four, the time was right for the world to be amazed by my sporting prodigy. Intoxicated by my expectations, I breezily brushed his first murmurs of protest aside. But by the time that we had found parking, I was starting to panic: "What do you mean you don't want to run? It will be fun boy". Unsure as to whether this was an order or an encouragement, my son turned to my wife; refuge for the still sane.

Fast forward to me leaning against one of the classroom walls, arms folded, bristling with indignation, as I watched other fathers' sons do what my boy was supposed to. I remember how he tugged at the knees of my jeans, confused and perplexed by my coldness. I remember my wife's brave, hotdog-armed attempts to resurrect my mood, and I remember how she looked at me searchingly, wondering where on earth her husband had gone.

We drove back a pretty subdued bunch, each in our own ways quite bewildered by the new bruises that we bore. Once home, the rest of the gang went about salvaging the tail end of the day, whilst I escaped to the bedroom, dishevelled and disoriented, imperious anger rapidly melting into uncertainty and shame.

Looking back, I realise that it was my first full dose of emotional training as a father and I can't say that I took my medication all that well. I know that my anger was over the top, but it's the memory of the way I rejected my four year-old son that still makes me wince.

As fathers, we have a special facility to guide our sensitive children. But as we get to know them, we also have several custom-made opportunities to review some of our narrow, ingrained assumptions about emotions, boys and girls. We have the chance to learn what it really means to 'be there' for our families.

Single Parents

Managing the balance between care and confrontation can be particularly difficult for single parents. However, if you are building your ability to talk with your child about his emotions, you can also talk about your need to wear two hats and alternate between care and confrontation. As your children get older you can even start to be more transparent about which end of the scale (care or confrontation) you find easiest, but because your child understands that both stances are in play, you can maintain a healthy balance.

"The secret lies not in avoiding life's inevitable frustrations and upsets, but in learning to recover from them. The faster the recovery, the greater the child's capacity for joyfulness."

– (Daniel Goleman, Social Intelligence) –

Chapter 14

Me and my friends

Your home is a social training ground

Because of their passionate, intense natures, friendships may be a source of both joy and heartache for a sensitive child. Parents often recognise their children's social vulnerabilities, but feel uncertain about the right steps to take. It's also very difficult to influence our children's social lives directly, which can lead to horrible feelings of helplessness and anguish. When your child is having difficulties, you might feel a strong impulse to march alongside her as a fierce playground bodyguard. A gratifying fantasy, but you know it can't be done.

Have you ever tried to make your child befriend another? Have you ever tried to make other children be nice to your child? It's never worked for me. Unfortunately, or perhaps fortunately, we have to guide and influence our child's social growth from a distance. But take heart, there are lots of things that a parent can do that have a powerful influence on this critical part of our children's lives. In fact, research shows that the way we relate to our children, our friendship in the home, contributes significantly to the health of outside friendships (Sroufe & Fleeson, 1988). We may have to be patient, but we don't have to feel powerless.

Infants begin dialoguing with their world from the word go. Babies and their parents develop patterns of interaction within all the feeding, cleaning, soothing and (hopefully) sleeping that make up those early months. They get to know each other, and babies get to know themselves in their worlds. Siegel (2004) describes how the 'parental gaze' develops an infant's neural capacity to give and receive love. Please don't underestimate the sacred investments that you are making simply by being there for your child.

Give your child a voice

Various writers have referred to *synchrony games* (Seligman, 2002). In these enjoyable exchanges, a parent deliberately mirrors her infant's actions or sounds. For example, just after a baby has banged on the table with her porridge spoon, a parent might 'reply' by taking up another spoon and joining in. These kinds of games teach very young children that they have a voice in the family, that what they say and do matters and can influence the ways others behave.

Then there's also good old-fashioned listening. By taking the time to listen to a child, we help her to practise expressing her opinions, ideas and feelings and we remind her that she has a unique voice in the world.

As you now know, I like to remind sensitive children that they have more than one way of being. I'm sure that you can remember times that you were confident, clever or funny and, unfortunately, times when you've felt like a real 'klutz'! As you trawl your memory banks, you can probably also identify the people and places that are likely to evoke these contrasting selves. Your child also has a multi-faceted character, and I think that it's good to let him know that you can see this.

Parents of sensitive children sometimes fall into the trap of 'speaking for' their children during social interactions. Perhaps it's because we want to protect them from feeling awkward, but this kind of ventrilo-quism can dampen children's ability to speak for themselves when they're with you. Where possible, resist the urge. If your child really battles with social events, encourage her to practise some specific behaviours (e.g. to make eye contact and then say hello) and then praise her efforts. Remember that, even when they're enjoying them-selves, the stimulation of social interaction can sometimes get too much for sensitive children. If this applies to your child, help him to understand this about himself, and to feel ok about saying when he's had enough.

Sensitive people sometimes hold onto the illusion that others are going to dismiss them because of their failings. The fact is, these so called 'failings' are potential points of connection not rejection. *In fact, people are often more able to relate to our struggles than to our successes.* But first, our children will have to learn how to put their struggles into words.

As I've said, many children (perhaps especially boys) hate the fact that they get emotional, and this becomes a 'no-go zone' when it comes to self-disclosures. Of course this usually ends up making things worse. Until these children have learned to give voice to what goes on in their chests, and to smile at their sensitivities, they remain emotionally tight. This also means that, as your child gets older, you will need to model a similar openness when it comes to your own emotional vulnerabilities.

Help your child to see the attributes of his big heart. You might want to remind him of his compassion, insight, self-discipline, or kindness to others.

Manipulation

Now and again I meet with parents who feel that they are being manipulated by their sensitive child. Sometimes only one of the parents (often the mother) seems to be a part of this dynamic as she tries to attend to her own irritation, an eyebrow raising-spouse and an upset child.

Perhaps it helps to realise that 'manipulation' happens when children don't feel able to ask for what they want in a more direct way. Children usually 'manipulate' to meet an *emotional need* that they either aren't consciously aware of or that they're embarrassed to openly admit. And golly, even adults can be completely chicken when it comes to expressing their emotional wants or needs.

As is so often the case with sensitive children, situations like this require that, without the use of shame, we use our insight and our words to make our children more aware of their internal, unconscious experiences. It is from this basis that new learning can begin:

> *"Paula, I can see that you're feeling nervous and that you want me to stay with you. But don't act like that. Use your words to tell me what you want."*

Dealing with the rough stuff

Many sensitive children don't deal with peer conflict very well. They can get uncertain, tense, or self-critical. Many either over-react or try to become invisible. And, of course, sometimes bullies hover around, ready to exploit these vulnerabilities.

When I ask sensitive children how they deal with aggressive children, many of them tell me that they've been advised to try and ignore the attacks. Whilst this strategy has its merits, it won't work in every situation. Olweus (1993) has found that that an anxious child, who remains passive or submissive when he is confronted, may well be targeted even more by bullies. In many cases then, telling a submissive child simply to ignore conflict can end up making the problem worse! I also think of a sensitive young man who said that his habit of masking what is important to him as an adult, began with his habit of ignoring teasing when he was a child. This is a costly price to pay.

Please remember that schools have to tackle bullying when it happens. I don't think that any child should be expected to deal with a bully without adult help. If a child could get out of being bullied on his own, he would. Situations of bullying require direct adult intervention.

But, for the long haul, it also seems vital for a sensitive child to explore and develop his assertive self. Many parents I've worked with have found that their children respond to specific coaching in this regard. What could your child say to defend himself in these situations? How should he go about recruiting adult help? What values justify and strengthen your child's stance? A nine year-old child felt quite empowered by the simple strategy of giving his tormentor one warning to stop before he called the teacher. This buffered the child from being called a 'tattle-tale' (he *had* given a warning), and it left him feeling like he had more control.

Perhaps it's the male in me, but I have also sometimes encouraged children to learn a few appropriate ways to defend themselves physically. Remember that perceived physical weakness is what places boys at risk for bullying. I don't think it's a bad thing for a child to learn how to get out of a wrist hold or a head lock. Surely we humans are allowed to have access to increasingly assertive ways of protecting ourselves? Shouldn't the moral act of 'turning the other cheek' emerge from a sense of choice rather than helplessness?

Once you and your younger child have settled on some realistic and concrete options, you might want to get into some role-playing. Acting out a range of scenes can help to give your child a better sense of who he needs to be when the heat is on. As Lerner (1993) points out, "Sometimes pretending is a form of experimentation or imitation that widens our experience and sense of possibility." (p.16) Some children need to get accustomed to the feeling of saying a loud, clear "No!".

Another way of empowering our children is to help them to think about the motives of the offending child. Why is the child saying what he's saying? What do the child's actions say about him? So many children who've been victims of teasing or bullying carry the idea that these things happen because there's something wrong with them. Preoccupied in this way, it's so difficult for children to lift their eyes and see the facts. Also, help your child to understand the difference between general scrapping (where it takes two to tango) and bullying (which is something that's *regularly* done to a *disempowered* child). If your child is being bullied, it really isn't his fault. Free him from any unwarranted guilt or shame that he's done something to deserve this treatment.

Social Skills

Sensitive children often feel uncomfortable around people who are unfamiliar to them. Being aware of a range of what are called *social skills* enables you to give your child concrete advice where necessary. It helps if you can breathe life into the skills by finding examples from your child's world. Remind him of times that he has already shown a desired skill. How did he do it? What would help him to repeat that skill in the week that lies ahead? You could also tell your child stories from your own experiences. How did you learn to be more assertive? How did you learn to laugh at yourself? What social skills are you busy learning? Are there any people, real or fictional, that you and your child can look to as role models in this regard? Use your imagination, have fun!

Describe your child's skills in the following areas:

- **Body language** (is your child looking at people during conversations, is she standing tall, and how often is she bringing out that winning smile?)

....

....

- **Voice quality** (does your child speak clearly and loudly enough to be heard? Does he relax his diaphragm enough to speak with a full tone?)

....

....

- **Conversation skills** (how is your child doing with greetings and introductions? Is she prepared to start conversations, to ask questions, and to choose topics of conversation? How is she at 'turn taking' during conversations?)

....

....

- **Friendship skills** (is your child offering help where suitable, or asking to join in? Is he expressing affection, giving compliments, or showing care when others are hurt or upset?)

....

....

- **Assertiveness** (is your child learning how to stick up for her rights? Where appropriate, does she know how to give appropriate warnings, or tell the teacher?)

  ....

  ....

Loving humour

I believe that learning to acknowledge and accept our sensitivities opens the door to that most excellent of social resources: humour. Laughter can stabilise our emotions, deflect social tension and connect people. But not all humour is healthy. Humour that is based on sarcasm, ridicule or bigotry tends to be spawned by covert insecurities. It's offensive, divisive and hurtful. It's favoured by people who are anxious about their status.

Is it not fair to say that people with the richest sense of humour have learnt to laugh at themselves? We feel drawn to these people because we recognise that their ability to laugh at their failings is a sign of inner strength. They accept themselves and so we sense that they will also be accepting of us. This, for me, is healthy humour. It names our own fragilities without condemnation. It is, in fact, an act of self-acceptance. It promotes love. It leaves us feeling more contained, and humanity leans towards our transparency.

Learning to laugh at our failings takes some doing. It's a mature skill. How can we help our children begin to experience its benefits? Well, for starters, we have to realise that healthy humour is based on self-respect. If your child is unsure of his intrinsic value he's really going to battle to raise a smile when he trips. Secondly, we need to be prepared to model the attitude. And it's difficult! I can't say that I'm particularly enjoying the slow betrayals of my 40 year-old body. But at the end of the day, when it comes to inner peace, I also know that accepting humour is more reliable than a hair restorer.

Let your children get used to speaking about their embarrassments. Loving homes that cradle this kind of exposure create space for the transformational effects of healthy laughter. I'm prepared to bet that your child will be more immune to teasing when her vulnerabilities have been rinsed in loving humour.

And of course it's not that I don't want your child to take himself seriously. In fact, people who *always* laugh at themselves are probably insecure about their strengths! For me, it's a matter of balance. Healthy, loving humour reminds us that we're a work in progress. It protects us from both the stress of perfectionism and the desolation of inadequacy.

McGhee (1999) suggests that playfulness fosters humour in children, and you might want to reflect on the amount of space your family schedule allows for play. Even if McGhee is wrong, I'd love you deliberately to have fun with your children.

"We have the right to be ridiculous"

– Bono of U2 speaks about family time –

Self-control enables interpersonal control

It's very difficult to be funny or friendly if one is feeling overwhelmed by anxiety or self-doubts. Realise then, that all the work we put into helping our sensitive children to accept and regulate their emotions *will* be accompanied by greater social confidence over time. When we are able to calm and control our emotions, we are better able to engage with others in more creative ways.

Children often remind me how difficult it can be when a group of more socially confident youngsters has you in their sights. A 14 year-old boy comes to mind. This sensitive, intelligent youngster had always preferred to work hard and alone. For some reason, he then had to do a lot of group work at school. Things hadn't gone well. He'd got frustrated with his group, others had seen him get worked up and the goading had started. The ways he acted on his frustrations only made things worse. Just like that, his year started to turn sour. He listened politely to my suggestions about what he could say and what he could do to defend himself, and said *"It won't work Rob."* He knew, in ways that I had forgotten, just how helpless and overwhelmed he felt when the pack decided to turn on him. He knew that, when the crunch came, words would fail him. It was important to stay loyal to his actual experiences, and to empower him in more personal, private ways. In a nutshell, we decided to use the metaphor of 'body armour'. Whenever he became the target of teasing, he would practise taking a calm diaphragm breath, as he imagined a breastplate of pride (complete with a coat of arms he'd designed) form over his heart. Once he'd taken his slow, deep breath, he chose to hold the thought 'almost holidays' (the school term was almost over) in his mind as a kind of protective helmet against the swirl of frustrated thoughts that threatened to overwhelm him. These two simple strategies left this youngster with an empowering secret. He was able to think more clearly and, because he didn't get caught up in any 'silly stuff', he got more support from the rest of his peers. The teasing pretty much stopped.

What about siblings?

Sibling relations are often overlooked, but their contribution to our children's social well-being can be huge. Across a lifetime, sibling relationships can outlast parent-child and even marital relationships. In later years, it's often our brothers and sisters who are there for us when times are tough.

Parents of sensitive children can come across some tricky situations when it comes to siblings. Sometimes there's the concern that a sibling will overshadow their sensitive child, perhaps because she's more outgoing, popular and conventionally successful than her sensitive sister. Or a father might worry that, because he has more in common with his other son, he's somehow short changing or neglecting his sensitive child. The reality is, at the end of the day they just aren't interested in the same things. And then there may be the concern that, because of her emotional nature, the sensitive child takes up more of her parents' time and attention, whilst the 'easier' children are left to sort their problems out for themselves.

Sometimes siblings get angry with sensitive children, because of the stress and difficulties that they raise. Of course, this only makes things worse. Siblings might ask their parents questions like; *"Why is Nigel always afraid of things?"* How should parents answer? I've also spoken with parents who've resolved to outlaw any talk of comparisons; of 'who's better than whom?' They don't want their conventionally less successful child to be hurt and to be left feeling inadequate.

The problem is; children *know* where they stand. They know who's the fastest, or the best at Maths. And, unfortunately, they also know who Dad prefers. Or, at least, they think they know; which has just about the same effect. I just don't think it's possible to protect a sensitive child by going covert or secretive about these things. Without intending to, I think that we give our sensitive child the message that his differences are shameful and irreconcilable. Our efforts at protecting our sensitive child backfire, but usually in underground, inaccessible ways. Perceptions and beliefs are held, but because they are emotionally charged, children aren't given the opportunity to talk them through. Thin and bony fingers of envy, resentment and inadequacy begin to grip the heart.

Again, it's so important for us to give our sensitive child the words and ways to occupy his world with confidence. Let your children compare themselves, but teach them how to do it well. Let them use these inevitable conversations as opportunities to polish the truth of their differences, and to celebrate the unique contribution that they make to the family. All of your children must learn to trust that their emotional needs will be met as they go about being themselves in the family. And, over time, a sensitive child will need to be able to talk openly about his emotional life with his brothers and sisters. That's intimacy.

Your sensitive child needs to live in a family story that has a special place for him. You will help him to occupy that place if there is more approval than criticism, and more confidence than doubt. In this way you train your child to engage an outside world that is often all about comparison and one-upmanship.

I can't think of a better training ground for a child to learn how to articulate and manage his emotional life, to discover and exercise his unique voice and gifts, than his family.

Try this!

- What kind of friend is your child? Help your children to understand that there are different styles of friendship and to value their own preferences.

- Every style has its downside. Leaders can be bossy, social butterflies can be fickle, and loyal supporters can be pushovers. Think up some scenarios to show your child that there are times when he might need to step out of his social preference; to speak when he'd prefer to keep quiet, to follow when she'd prefer to lead, to join in when he'd prefer to keep his distance.

- When one of our children is in distress, it's only natural for us to focus our attention and energy on their needs. But do remember to preserve some space for your other children. Make sure that they also have a chance to check in with you, to express their own voices. Watch that your children aren't getting too stuck in a particular family role. Everyone in the home needs a chance to both give and receive support.

- Using Chapter 16 as a prompt, look for opportunities to talk about the ways each of your children's strengths contributes to the overall health of the family. What kinds of family situations draw on these strengths?

- Encourage your children to celebrate each other's strengths. Expect a high frequency of the phrase 'thank you' between family members.

- It can be horrible when our children argue about who is 'king of the hill'. And they will. But still, these times are opportunities for your children to experience such social buffeting with you close at hand. Under your guidance, your children can learn what it takes to speak for themselves, and to turn away when they aren't being appropriately respected.

- Remember that 'common interests' aren't the only basis for intimacy. Children (and perhaps especially teens) love it when parents show a genuine interest in their alternative points of view. Like any healthy ecosystem, families thrive when variation is held dear.

I can remember feeling a horrible mixture of dread, guilt and anger every time we went camping. Of course I loved my family, and I hated disappointing them, but I just wasn't into the whole fishing/boating thing. A part of me wanted to say "Please leave me behind!" whilst another just wanted to weep. Things really changed when my parents encouraged me to bring my painting materials along. They asked me to use my ability to capture some of these times that were so precious to them. They still keep one of my paintings on their mantle piece.

When it comes to friendships, many sensitive children opt for quality over quantity. But nevertheless, these few select relationships are usually a source of great assurance and satisfaction.

As we look to respect our children's feelings and to encourage their 'voices' at home, we teach them to trust in their own style of friendship and to value their innate wisdom, loyalty and compassion.

"A child's peer style – how he relates to his friends – is a combination of two primary factors: that child's basic temperament and how a child is treated at home."

– Taffel & Blau –

Chapter 15

Healthy motivation

Manageable challenges help to activate positive arousal

You know that there's a world out there that your child just has to face. This is not just because it's inevitable, but also because the world offers up challenges that are vital for growth and emotional health. Sensitive, self-doubting children can be caught in a trap of inactivity, where they duck opportunities for growth and fun in favour of the safe confines of underachievement, romance novels or play station games. These children are in real danger of being half of what they could be. They are unsure of their abilities and they shrink back at the possible pain of failure. Sadly, it's quite easy to avoid the threat of failure: you just opt out. You keep your abilities in the deep freeze.

How can we provide contexts that will motivate our children to risk using the talents that God has given them?

Teach your child to focus on what he can control

When children and teens talk to me about their goals, I often find that they'll say something like *"I want to come first"*, or *"I want to get 80%"*, or *"I want to score a hundred runs"*. Now, as I've said, I love it when children succeed. But at the same time, I want children, and perhaps especially sensitive children, to focus on what they can control. As wonderful as the above goals are, they're not directly under the children's control. They are what can be called outcome goals. They come at the tail end of a whole sequence of steps that each child has to take. When a child only holds outcome goals in her mind, it's very easy for her motivation to become *threat based*. If you are working hard and thinking all the time, *"I have to get an A"* chances are that your study fuel is primarily being sourced from the fear of *not* getting the A, and all the shame that goes with that! Its avoidance based motivation and it sets high achieving children up for a nasty roller-coaster ride. Success brings relief, rather than joy, and failure brings despair.

So I ask children to tell me about the things they have to *do* to make these outcomes most likely to happen. What, how, when, and where do the children need to learn or practise? These are preliminary steps that children can actually control. They give children the best chance of reaching the outcomes they want.

Establishing focus goals

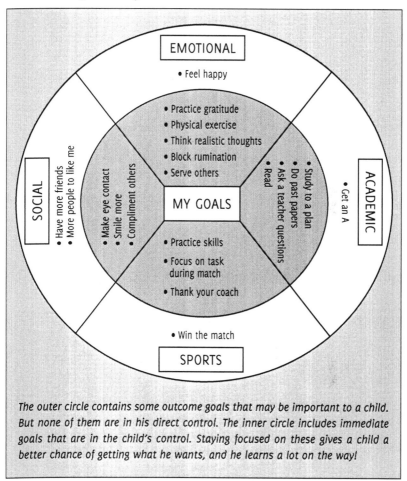

The outer circle contains some outcome goals that may be important to a child. But none of them are in his direct control. The inner circle includes immediate goals that are in the child's control. Staying focused on these gives a child a better chance of getting what he wants, and he learns a lot on the way!

Teaching children to keep their focus on what they can control (or *manageable challenges*) reminds them to keep working on their skills. It helps to activate an empowering, positive arousal.

Sports studies show that children respond well when coaching focuses on fun, effort and personal improvement. Effective coaches respond to mistakes with encouragement and a specific focus on the skills that the child needs to learn. Children coached in these ways feel more confident, more motivated, and they practise harder (Larson, 2000).

When we keep our children focussed on the skills they need to learn, they are more likely to understand that prowess results from practise. Children who receive this kind of feedback are more likely to persevere. They are motivated by feelings of challenge. By contrast, comments like "Well done for getting an A" keep the child's focus on an outcome that is actually beyond his control (unless he marks his own work). He is again at risk of stepping onto a tightrope of performance anxiety where he works hard because he's afraid of not getting an A next time (threat).

Look out for opportunities to praise the development of specific skills rather than results alone. Let your child realise that your attention and approval are focussed on her efforts:

"Well done – five wickets! I saw that you kept your arm nice and high."

"You danced beautifully! You watched the teacher and you listened so nicely to the music. That seemed to help you keep in time."

"Great picture! I could see you really concentrating and making small pencil strokes with your crayons."

"Bad luck buster! Boy, that guy ran a good race today. But well done for setting a new personal best! I can see that your interval training is paying off on those last hundred metres."

Handling competition

During competition, we normally compare ourselves with others. For many sensitive children, this generates stressful, threat-based arousal, which can result in a loss of focus and creative energy. Children get stuck on who's doing better than whom and they start to become very self-conscious. They start to dread how horrible they are going to feel if, or when, they lose. Their focus is all wrong. Help your child to keep her focus on her own game plan. She can practise some of the strategies you have already read about (strong thoughts, imagery, cue cards, diaphragm breathing) while she keeps bringing her attention back to things that she can control (watch the ball, move your feet, compliment your opponent).

Perfectionism

As with many attributes of the sensitive child, *perfectionism* has to be seen as potentially both good and bad. If your child is wired in this way, then he's probably always going to want things to be done properly, to have a sense of excellence when he sets himself goals. There's nothing wrong with this and I don't think that we can really ask a child not to care about things that he naturally cares about. But I've found that some children who have been called perfectionist are actually what I would call *faultist*. It's as though they are constantly distracted and upset by errors or imperfections in the things that they do. If a child has a natural tendency to be a perfectionist, I try to teach her to focus on the positive side of her passion by asking, *"What is it that you need to do to achieve this great aim? How will you know when you've got there? How will you encourage yourself when things don't go smoothly? How will you celebrate when you've reached your aim?"*

Managing ourselves

Studies suggest that children tune out when we constantly go on about how capable they are. It seems that our children are better motivated when we focus our praise and encouragement on their efforts. Also, when your child tells you that an upcoming challenge is going to be tough, don't necessarily disagree with him (*"Don't worry, you can easily run that far!"*, or *"But you're much better than Susan, sweetheart"*). Children are more likely to persevere when you have helped them to build up the focus and determination they think they'll need to take on what they see as a real challenge.

Although we might be thrilled when our cautious child actually starts to attempt something, it's probably best to control our enthusiasm a bit. For one thing, children practise better when our feedback and encouragement is intermittent. They need time to practise on their own. Also, we want to be sure that our excitement doesn't drown out the natural curiosity and motivation brewing in our children. So don't splash out on all the latest equipment when your child's interest first starts to bud. Stay cool. Walk in step.

Integrity

It can be especially important for sensitive children to feel proud of their behaviour. So, when you are looking at behaviours that are in your child's control, include actions that build your child's sense of integrity. Whether it's thanking the referee after the game, encouraging team mates, or practising hard, let your child know that you value demonstrations of character, regardless of the score line.

Celebrate

It's strange how 'lemon-mouthed' we can be about our successes. Perhaps we worry that something bad is going to happen if we allow ourselves to get too happy. If this applies to you, please don't pass your reservations onto your child. In fact I'd like you to help your child to *celebrate* her achievements. When we celebrate, we produce endorphins in our bodies. We feel exuberant, charged and energised, able to conquer the world. This feeling envelops our whole body. Also, we are left with a memory that propels us forward with more vigour. They say that success breeds success. But really, it's only the achievements that we cherish that stay fertile.

Beware of burnout

There seems to be so much more formal competition nowadays, and it hits our children earlier than I ever remember. Even in so-called "off seasons" many of my young clients are busy with strength and skills-building exercises. When it comes to training, the theory seems to be 'more is better'.

I guess this is wonderful. I'm always delighted and inspired by the achievements of these young people. All the same, we have to be careful. Sensitive, hard-working and perfectionist children can be at risk of burnout.

> "As a talented sportsman, Marc was so busy, week in and week out. We could see that he was getting tired, but he would just get angry with us whenever we suggested that he was taking on too much. He sets himself such high standards, and he hates feeling that he's letting anyone down at school. I don't think I'll ever forget the morning that he lifted his head off the pillow, looked up at me and said that he didn't want to get out of bed ever again. He looked so drained! We all knew that something had to change."

Warning signs

Parents, here are some of the warning signs of burnout in young people:

- physical exhaustion
- sleep disturbance
- a drop-off in performance
- loss of interest or energy
- distancing from others
- increased conflict with parents or coaches
- increased negativity ("I won't win", "What's the point?", "Who cares?")

We have to watch that, as talented as they are, our children don't over-invest their identities in their sports. Because of this, some of the children I have seen have struggled when hit by long-term injuries. It's as though they felt horribly empty and lost without their sport. Some over-focussed children need to be reminded of the value of friends and simple, everyday fun.

We might also have to stop ourselves from getting too excited for our children, particularly if school bursaries, or some other harbinger of professional sport, begin to flicker. And, where necessary, hand back the reins. Researchers tell us that children who have a say over their activities (what, where, how much) are buffered from burnout.

Children who have just done a lot of competing might need to remember what drew them to the activity in the first place: the pleasure of hitting a ball, singing a song, or drawing a bow across some strings. And perhaps because the fantastical world of play is activated I believe that budding sports kids can learn things in backyard games with friends that they'll never access during formal coaching. It's during the timeless hours of free play that our children imitate their heroes, and allow themselves to dream wonderful dreams.

The best strategy for enjoying life is to develop whatever skills one has and to use them as fully as possible.

— Jackson & Csikszentmihalyi —

Chapter 16

Help your child to discover her strengths

Our children come to know who they are through the relationship that they share with us.

Some time ago I listened to a father reflect on his sensitive child in what I recognise as a fairly typical, bitter-sweet way. He was able to recount a blend of wonderful and perplexing stories about his boy. One of the moments that stood out for this Dad, was the time his son stopped in the middle of a competitive sports match to tend to one of his fallen friends. Not recommended by many coaching manuals, but somehow noteworthy, just the same.

So much of parenting seems to depend on how we notice our children. And I confess that my "Watch this, Dad" stamina is often horribly feeble. Even though I love the little guy, I find it hard to be enthusiastic about my son's fifth handstand. But I realise that it's a currency that all my children crave and that, over time, it acts as a powerful influence on their growth. In many ways, our children come to know who they are through the relationship that they share with us. They see themselves through our eyes. Our perceptions become their truths.

With this in mind, think about the fact that many of us spend lots of time dwelling on our children's *weaknesses*. Several surveys have shown that when parents go over their children's school reports, bad marks get far more talk time than good marks. Perhaps this is natural; we absolutely love our children and because of this we worry about the things that seem to be holding them back. We fuss and grumble because we care. Indifference would be worse. But we have to be careful. Because worry keeps us focussed on what is wrong, it can cause us to overlook or downplay our children's talents. Because our children track our attention, they could so easily join us in this negative preoccupation and end up devaluing the things that they *can* do.

Best-selling author Marcus Buckingham says that we simply have to take our natural talents seriously, because these are the areas that contain the most scope for growth, success and personal satisfaction. His claims are backed by research into the lives of successful people from all walks of life who, it turns out, have risked investing in the things that they are naturally good at. In this troubled world many of us have very little clue about the things that we do spontaneously well. Instead, we are experts on our weaknesses. We waste precious years picking at these shame spots, hoping against hope that we can transform them into strengths.

For Buckingham this is all wrong! For starters, it's highly unlikely that we will turn a weakness into a genuine strength. Of course we can improve our weaknesses, but in slow, frustrating and often unreliable ways. By contrast, investing in our God-given talents brings rapid growth and achievement. Instead of feeling drained we feel invigorated because what we are doing *fits* us. When we invest in our natural capacities we learn the related skills with ease and begin to perform at consistently high standards.

I must admit that, until recently, I thought of talents in quite narrow ways. Perhaps because of our school systems, or the kinds of people that the media spotlights, I've tended to see 'talent' as being about athleticism, intelligence, musical ability or beauty. All of these leave me feeling a bit flat and inadequate. And because these kinds of talents have been colonised by a competitive world, I can get anxious when my children don't seem to measure up somehow.

Look closer, say the experts. Look at the things that are woven into the fabric of your child's being. What are the things that she spontaneously does? What are his instinctive, day-to-day reactions? What are the things that she loves to do, regardless of your prompting? We need to give fresh awareness to those things that we may have taken for granted, things that just seem to be a part of who we know our child to be. Research psychologist, Dr Clifton, said that any personality quirk that can be put to good use should be seen as a talent. This means that we can (or should) start to appreciate our child's natural determination, sense of humour, imagination, friendliness, or responsibility, and so on. As you can see, it's so easy to overlook these kinds of talents. Very few awards are handed out for the ability to argue. As a loving parent, you can do so much for your child by helping him to see that his natural ways are studded with personal abilities that he can build his future around. When we recognise and bless these intimate aspects of our children, they are able to feel loved for who they are, rather than for who we'd like them to be.

Many sensitive children hate the fact that they get emotional. However, if we take a few steps back and start to look at emotions as a kind of personal energy, then we can start to see the attributes that come with this unique 'juice'. Perhaps your child can start to understand that he doesn't have to be ashamed of his intense and sometimes overwhelming emotions. With his nature may come enthusiasm, creativity, empathy, or the ability to stand up for what's right.

Try this!

- Perhaps you and your spouse could select and tell each other three stories that you think are typical of your child. Then take some time to discern the talents that might be embedded in these stories. How would your child's friends describe her? What qualities do they find attractive?

- Be aware that newborn talents can sometimes look quite ugly. Anyone who's raised a child with a talent for determination or competitiveness will testify to this. So don't be surprised if your child's early talents (e.g. caution or sense of humour) are disguised as behaviours that really annoy you. You need to ask yourself whether these habits could be useful in any way, and if so, what positive word could you use to describe the behaviour?

- Look for opportunities to talk to your child about the talents you have noticed. Tell him about the times that you have seen him using the talent. Once you have given his ability a word, help him to understand its meaning and to own it.

- Help your child to see how these vital parts of herself can be assets in her life, both now and in her future. Give your child opportunities to exercise her talents in the home (e.g. care, fairness, leadership, forgiveness). And then, how could your child continue to develop her talents outside of the home?

- Buckingham says that a talent doesn't qualify as a strength until one has put in 'the hard yards' and learnt how to make the most of it consistently. Even talents require practise. Also, you may need to help your child to see what it means to use her talent in wise, helpful ways.

- Self-knowledge is a life-long process. Don't give your child the idea that you have unearthed all of his talents. He is going to continue to grow in many ways.

- As we learn about our areas of strength we also become more aware of those things that we just don't seem to be good at. You might even find that, as your child learns to trust in her strengths, she becomes more accepting of her imperfections. But be cautious about identifying areas of weakness with your child. In terms of development, he is not yet finished and he will no doubt continue to surprise himself, and you, for many years to come.

- Remember, it's not that we ignore our children's weaknesses or immaturities. Rather, we approach these areas with the aim of ensuring that they won't block or frustrate our children's abilities to fully realise their strengths. Even if a talented entrepreneur doesn't have a flair for accountancy, it really helps if he has some grasp of the basics.

I'm not saying that we should allow our children to simply drop the things they don't like. Many school classrooms would start to echo if we did. One of the key benefits of enabling our children to pursue their passions is that they learn how to cope with setbacks. Our children must know not to walk away too soon. And, of course, there are some things that all of us have to do. That's life. However, I believe that an awareness of your child's emerging strengths helps you to encourage and motivate her with greater insight and compassion. If marathons were compulsory, I know that I'd prefer a support team that understood that I'm no natural and praised my efforts along the way. On the other hand, I also know that I'd get really grumpy and resistant if my team was anxious or offended because I didn't seem to be enjoying myself. Children feel inadequate when we imply that they should love something that they don't. They feel strong and proud when we recognise that they have made an effort to do something even though it goes against the grain.

Trusting in, and enabling our children's talents takes a certain kind of courage. We have to take a stand against the *shoulds* and *oughts* of the world. We have to recognise that there are many ways to live a good life, and that our child's best shot at fulfilment comes, ultimately, from investing in his unique design.

> *Our sensitive child can sometimes be a real pain. He can be quite a 'worry pot', but what really bugs me is how he gets something in his mind and then just won't let it go! Whether it's something he 'needs' from the shops, or something that he doesn't want to do, he can grumble and fuss until he gets his own way. We often give in to him, but it can be so irritating.*
>
> *Until recently, my standard response would be to tell him to "Stop obsessing!" But after thinking about this whole strengths thing I realised that he will probably always be single minded (his Dad's actually like that) and that this can be a good thing in life. So I spoke with him again, but instead I used the words 'single minded' and 'determined' and we thought together about the ways that this helps him both now and in the future. I did say, though, that I wanted him to control this strength, and that I would still get angry with him if he didn't give me a break and practise patience sometimes.*

Signs of talent

Look out for some of the following signs of a talent in action (Seligman, 2002, p.160):

- A sense of authenticity ("This is the real me")
- A feeling of excitement while displaying it, particularly at first
- A rapid learning curve as the strength is first practised
- Continuous learning of new ways to use the strength
- Invigoration rather than exhaustion while using the strength

Take a moment to describe the things that your child often like to do. Then look for a word that captures an underlying strength. Use the suggestions below to get you thinking:

The things my child likes to do	Strength word
1.	
2.	
3.	
4.	
5.	

Suggestions

- To keep my thinking clear, I like to divide strengths up into personal growth and social ability (some strengths help us to achieve personal success, while others help us to get on with others).

- Here are some of the talents that I've often seen in sensitive children: creativity, curiosity, love of learning, wisdom, integrity, kindness, fairness, social responsibility, forgiveness, prudence, gratitude and spirituality.

- Here are some of the more unusual strengths that often seem particular to sensitive children: drive to achieve, analytical, competitive, disciplined, focussed and principled.

Strengths-based research also provides an important tip for parents of multi-talented children: remember that children will naturally enjoy expressing their talents. You 'just' need to facilitate opportunities for him to grow his talent. If you find yourself pleading with him to follow through on a commitment because he's 'good at it' the chances are that it may not be a true talent. Capable children might be able to do many things, but only the things they spontaneously enjoy can qualify as talents.

It can be frustrating and sad to see a child walk away from an activity that you cherish and, worse still, that he's good at. But no matter how well he does, long-term progress is going to get tricky if his inner fuel remains unlit. Your child's energy, creativity and personal satisfaction reside in his strengths.

Know your own strengths and weaknesses

Because our strengths are such a key part of who we are, it's important to acknowledge how they contribute to our parenting. And, of course, we don't want to live under the oppressive belief that we should be good at every aspect of this challenging life assignment. We're allowed to have our weak spots. In fact, it's probably important to acknowledge that, as parents, we aren't the complete article. Just like everyone else in the family, we are always learning.

Sometimes, couples get stuck because one way of being a parent is privileged over another. In these situations, even a good thing can turn bad: strengths can become *noxious* because they aren't regularly diluted by other points of view. Without diversity, homes become overly controlled, or chaotic, or competitive, or passive, and so on. Others' natural strengths are devalued, and family members are enticed to live in monochromatic ways. For me, a sign of this kind of imbalance is where a parent lacks confidence in his or her style of parenting, and where key decisions are constantly deferred to one partner.

Take a moment to identify your own strengths as a parent. Remember, these are the aspects of parenting that seem to fit who you are. They come naturally to you and people who know you recognise that you are gifted in those areas. Where appropriate, do the same for your partner. (Here are some strength words to prompt your thinking: wisdom, empathy, playfulness, humour, responsibility, encouragement, leadership.)

My parenting strengths:	My partner's parenting strengths:
1.	1. ....
2.	2. ....
3.	3. ....
4.	4. ....

Look for opportunities in the days ahead to acknowledge the special strengths that your partner brings into the home.

You cannot be anything you want to be –
but you can be a lot more of who you already are.

– Tom Rath –

Chapter 17

Children of purpose

*Having a purpose satisfies a child's need
to belong to something bigger than himself.*

In his book *Noble Purpose* (2005), William Damon describes the enormous richness that we enjoy when our efforts are guided by a meaningful focus. Something special happens when we give ourselves over to a large-scale project, particularly when that project benefits others. For many sensitive children it can be very important to have a sense of their virtue and to be involved in something 'good'.

When we are involved in something we find meaningful that makes a difference to the world, we have a purpose. Damon feels that even children benefit from having a sense of purpose. It satisfies a child's need to belong to something bigger than himself. It promotes a sense of significance and meaning in an often all-too confusing world. Purpose, Damon argues; "endows a person with joy in good times and resilience in hard times."

Mary had to move schools again at the end of last year. We felt terrible because we know how long it took her to settle the last time. But we had no choice really. The first couple of weeks were really gloomy. Although Mary was trying to be her usual sweet self I could tell that she was unhappy and I was starting to feel more and more guilty and angry with my husband because of the move.

Although the rest of the year was still difficult for Mary, I really saw a change in her when she started to go on the school's outreach programme every Friday afternoon. Mary has always been naturally kind and she is wonderful with younger children. Some of the stories she brought back were heartbreaking, but she so enjoyed getting to know the kiddies at the Home. And they loved her! It was also a great way for her to link up with some of the other girls from her school.

Dr Stephen Post has studied what happens to people when they give of themselves to others. He has found that generous behaviour reduces depression and risk of suicide in teenagers. He has also found that the mental and physical health of teenagers is generally boosted when they are involved in helping others. These benefits also last all the way into late adulthood. Post has been quoted as saying: "It's abundantly clear from a number of studies that people who live generous lives also live happier lives." Interestingly, Post goes on to say that the benefits of giving lie not in the action itself, but in "the love or caring underlying the action" (*The Witness*, 13/08/07).

Fostering purpose in our children

- Our wealth and success will not necessarily foster a sense of purpose in our children. Through our own commitments and priorities, we need to model the fact that there is more to life than chasing bread.

- Many sensitive teenagers have withdrawn from their worlds to such an extent that they are chronically bored. Everyone gets bored, but when this sets in as a life theme, watch out! Bored teens are at risk for all sorts of things that are not life enhancing, from shallow entertainment to more dangerous forms of sensation-seeking such as substance abuse and vandalism (Vandovich). Bored children and teens tend to dwell on themselves and their private experiences. This bramble of introspection stops children from moving forward and can leave them feeling empty and dissatisfied.

- By contrast, interest-filled or purposeful youngsters tend to grow in confidence, they begin to trust themselves more and to look to the future with enthusiasm and optimism.

- Commitments should be meaningful to children. You don't want to get to the point where you are dragging a reluctant teenager around who keeps asking "Why do we need to do this stuff?" At the same time, studies show that even purposeful youngsters sometimes moan about their commitments. Most of us are the same about our work demands, and yet few of us would actually be happier if we lost the daily challenges that work provides. Do listen to your child. Don't let resentments build, but, at the same time, perhaps you don't need to be too thrown by the occasional early morning protest.

- Sadly, huge gaps exist between the communities of our country, gaps that have become breeding grounds for suspicion, generalisation and fear. Our impulse is often to protect our children from people who are different from us. Not only can this entrench prejudices, but it also prevents children and teenagers from expressing the wonderful passion and idealism that seems to come so naturally to the young.

  As a further complication, I find that many sensitive children are real techno-junkies. Of course it's great that they learn to use modern gadgets but, at the same time, don't many of these things end up insulating our children from the real world? Isn't it perhaps just too easy for a reserved child to hide behind a computer or iPod?

- There are so many ways that we can contribute to our communities and, as Damon indicates, it is never too early (or too late) to start. But, as Larson (2000) shows, many children benefit from being part of a project that includes older teenagers or adults. Within such projects, children learn important problem-solving skills, and they are exposed to challenges that they perhaps wouldn't have the confidence to tackle on their own. They are given opportunities to practise their *initiative*.

- Such projects are rarely found within the confines of a school day. Other channels need to be explored. Larson says that initiative develops when a child takes on projects that take time and effort, involve obstacles and setbacks, but are enjoyable. How could your child use his strengths to contribute to his community? What activities could bring him into contact with positive role models? Search for overlaps between your family's values or beliefs, your child's natural strengths and the needs that are out there. What can your family commit to for a season? Who will be responsible for what? Take some steps of faith.

- Encourage your child's spiritual development. Look for opportunities to talk about the big picture, about what really counts at the end of the day. Help your child to participate in organisations that foster a sense of meaning (e.g. church, wildlife societies, charities and youth projects).

....

Our children are sometimes overwhelmed by the challenges and dangers of modern life. A clarifying sense of purpose can be a powerful antidote to the fear, hopelessness and apathy that many bewildered children feel. Developing a sense of purpose helps sensitive children to see through their emotional mists and move towards visible, valued reference points. Children of purpose stay connected with their worlds. They experience hope. They keep growing.

"Don't aim at success – the more you aim at it and make it a target, the more you are going to miss it. For success, like happiness, cannot be pursued, it must ensue ... as the unintended side-effect of one's personal dedication to a cause greater than oneself."

– Victor Frankl –

Chapter 18

Love and Fear

"Our children arouse two of our
most compelling motives:
love and fear."

There are few things that will mobilise our hearts more powerfully than our own children. Their well-being, their ways, and their futures are inextricably imprinted into our own experiences of life. Our children are, in so many ways, vital parts of who we are.

Because we care so much, we will probably find that our children arouse two of our most compelling motives: love and fear. Many of our parenting choices and actions will be prompted by the vast love that we hold for our children, but some will emanate from the fears that we carry, for our children and for ourselves. I don't think that it's possible, or even desirable, for us not to worry about our children. But I do think that parenting can be sabotaged when fears are either overriding or masked.

If our parenting is dominated by fear, it will be very difficult for us to give our sensitive children enough scope to grow into themselves. Because fear prompts such a strong need to control, our children's challenges will leave us overly rattled, our patience will be too thin and we will be too scared to trust in their emerging strengths. Even worse, our fears could make us lose out on any number of smiles, hugs, wrestling matches and laughs during those few crazy years of early family life.

We probably are going to worry about our children. But we have to be smart about our fears. We have to know them and know how to rein them in. Our covert, or unrecognised fears, can end up being quite destructive for our children, especially if they don't exactly fit the mould. We live in a world etched by powerful currents of conformity. We are all seduced into singing the same songs. But many sensitive children have been given alternative scores to sing. If we want our children to be able to contribute in full voice, there are going to be many times that we will need to have the courage to applaud their divergence.

Of course we must be realists. The world tends to scowl at difference, and we don't want our children to waddle out as strange, sitting ducks. We must prepare them for life. But at the same time, parenting is not simply about what's out there. We might also need to wrestle with our own implicit hopes and dreams. Perhaps a part of us might wish that our sensitive children were more 'normal', and we are reluctant to set this aside as an ultimate, unspoken goal. And again there are the fears that we have for our contrary children, fears of the pain they might have to face and fears of who they might become. The thing is, beyond words, and perhaps even beyond their conscious awareness, our children probably 'know' about our fears for them. And this kind of knowledge can end up shaping vast tracts of their lives. Their deep-down sense of confidence can be blighted by our own misgivings. This can profoundly influence the choices that they end up making as adults.

If we make an effort to identify our fears, their potentially negative influence can be contained. Awareness of our fears helps us to be responsive rather than reactive. We give our better wisdom a chance to come into play.

Some time ago I met Stephen, a wonderfully talented, sensitive teenager. Because of his abilities, he'd just been admitted to a top-notch traditional high school. Unfortunately, at this early stage, he was troubled and unhappy. He'd battled to adjust to the rather rigid demands of his new community and he'd come in for a fair amount of flak from the other students. Now, as I've said, Stephen is a capable guy. He certainly didn't want to throw in the towel. But all the same, he was feeling quite lost. His parents also didn't know which way to turn. One part of them wanted to take their son out of the school straight away, whilst another part of them felt frustrated and embarrassed that their son couldn't just 'fit in'. Well, in his own way, Stephen ended up thriving at the school. I believe that a key reason for his recovery was the brave and wise stance that his parents adopted in the face of his distress. Taking hold of their own anxieties, and being supportive but patient, Stephen's parents were able to show him that it was possible to stay at the school without losing his identity. They demonstrated a confidence in their son's ability to forge his own path within the culture of his school. They didn't ask Stephen to change, but they did ask him to think about, and experiment with, the best ways for him to participate. I have no doubt that this tough experience has boosted Stephen's sociability enormously. But I also know that he wouldn't have done it if his parents hadn't checked their fears enough to express the implicit faith that they have in their son.

As strange as it may sound, I think that we often have to remind ourselves to free up the love that we have for our sensitive children. Carr (2002) reminds us that love "encompasses offshoots like hope, curiosity, trust, and delight" (p.268). I sincerely hope that the ideas expressed in this book might help you to douse some of your anxieties and feel more excited about your child's possibilities. I know that, if you feel more able to slow down and relax, you will be better able to tap into the deep well of love that you have for your child. Of course, it's not about simply letting go. You have to guide your child towards her world and she will need your wisdom and support in huge dollops. But I believe that a special kind of magic happens when our children grasp, beyond words, that we delight in them and that we have faith in their ability to live out their own lives.

Under the influence of fear

How can we tell when fear's got us by the tail? Here are some sure signs:

- We find that we're often angry with our child, and that we end up saying critical or derogatory things to her.

- We keep dwelling on our child's problems.

- We keep dwelling on what our child 'should' or 'ought' to be doing.

- We become rigid about house rules

- We push our children too hard

- We keep searching for what the 'experts' have to say.

- We are overly serious when we're with our children. We've stopped laughing with them.

- We feel overly guilty or anxious when we think we've 'blown it' as parents.

- We get anxious when our child is with other adults.

- We over-monitor our child's interactions with other children.

- We keep telling our child to 'be careful'.

- We continuously let our children duck the consequences of their actions.

"There is no fear in love" (1 John 4:18)

The fierceness of love

Psychologist Dr Stephen Gilligan reminds us that there's a certain 'fierceness' in love. Loving someone well requires us to fight for their best interests, to promote their strengths and encourage their dreams.

But if we want our loved ones to reach their potential, and to lead fulfilling lives, we will have to make demands on them from time to time. Because sensitive children can get very emotional, this is sometimes fairly daunting. They don't always like to be pushed out of their comfort zones and, as parents, it can be tempting to follow the path of least resistance.

So we need to monitor ourselves. If we've allowed our sensitive children to sneak past certain social obligations because we are afraid of their big emotions, we may just end up inadvertently letting them down. Even if they do get upset and angry, we must still expect our children to learn about manners, to help around the house, and to discover what it means to push themselves. Without this, our children could leave home with muscles that are simply too soft. They won't be able to fight for themselves.

If you think that you have gone passive on some of these principles; be brave, find your loving fierceness, and expect your sensitive child to give her best self some regular workouts.

The Vulnerability of Love

Perhaps 'belief' is too strong a word; so let me rather say that I have the *suspicion* that the children we receive are specifically designed to teach us something important about ourselves. Simply by being who they are, our children will stretch us into many unfamiliar and often uncomfortable places. They'll push our buttons, and we may find ourselves reacting in ways that we'd never have believed possible, back in the cool, calm waters of child-free life.

In families, there is little room for faking. We just can't maintain our poses for that long. All that we are, from the elegant to the infantile, is called into play. Our cherished goals, forgotten yearnings, hidden doubts and insecurities are all likely to be stepped on in the closeness of family life. And our children's small feet can be unwittingly accurate in this regard.

Love asks us to be open to these intimate events, to bring our subterranean parts out into the sun. Exposing our secret selves to the light of real relationships can be scary, but it is one of the great chances we get to become more human. As we give our loved ones permission to truly know us, we also get repeat opportunities to grow. When it comes to parenting, there's no such thing as distance learning.

Acknowledging and reflecting on our own emotional needs can leave us feeling quite vulnerable. But I do think that the practice allows us, at the very least, the occasional rueful smile.

The other day I popped my head into my three year-old daughter's room, keen to connect. She looked up and saw me at the door. But then she simply looked back down and, in the most matter-of-fact manner, said "Go away, I'm playing a game".

Steal a moment just to look at your child. Renowned prosthetic surgeon, Dr Paul Brand, reminds us that the best engineers and surgeons in the world could not add one improvement to your child's thumb, let alone her hands. And it's those hands that must make something of opportunity. It's those hands that must fight for what is right. Those are the hands that will hold the next generation. Teach them, sure. But let's strive to practise this with the lightness of laughter, the fierceness of purpose, and the stillness of trust.

"Wealth is not an absolute. It is relative to desire. Every time we seek something we cannot afford, we grow poorer ... And every time we feel satisfied with what we have, we can be counted as rich ..."

– Alain de Botton –

Afterword

Parents who have consulted with me for years still grapple, from time to time, to know what to do with their children's sensitivity. Different life phases bring different challenges, and the difficulties inherent in having a sensitive nature can take on unexpected faces. As a parent it's sometimes hard not to feel downhearted when you find yourself marshalling your energies with a 'Here we go again' heaviness.

One such parent felt a moment of swamping despair when her tearful son phoned from a distant university. He had seemed so strong, so positive, and he'd been sailing through his academic programme. But this loving, amazing mother was able to put down the phone with a sense of elation and justifiable pride. Not because her son was an emotional rock but because, during the course of the telephone conversation, he took responsibility for identifying the ways he was going to recover and regroup, leaving her free to simply affirm and support. Although she felt for her son, the problem remained his. She knew that the home relationship had left him with the tools to cope, the tools to keep growing, and an abiding sense of being recognised and cherished.

You can see from this story that I want young people to learn how to take stock and keep moving. It's not simply about staying happy: life's too complex for that. Some challenges are simply going to wash over our defences and clean us out. So sometimes it's going to be necessary for our children to reinvent themselves in creative, constructive ways. I believe that two abilities will be vital to this process: your child's ability to enter into her emotional experiences and, at the ends of these corridors of the heart, to pause, and remember who she is. In both matters, your guidance and your love can make all the difference.

Appendix

Establishing new sleep routines

Try this!

- I've seldom come across a child who's changed sleeping habits easily, so be prepared for at least one or two nights of unhappiness. But know that, with perseverance and perhaps some creativity, most children are able to acclimatise fairly quickly.

- Be careful not to shame your child into change (e.g. *"You should be old enough to sleep in your own bed by now"*). I suggest that you give your child neutral, practical reasons for the change. These might include your own needs (*"Honey, I'm just not getting enough sleep right now. I need you to get used to staying in your own bed"*) or an upcoming change in your child's routine (*"You are going to have to start going to sleep the same time as your sister because you are also going to big school now"*).

- It makes sense to follow our children's advice when they say that some small change (e.g. a night light, heavier curtains or an audio book) will help them to feel more settled at bedtime.

- Some parents have found that children are more ready to stay in their rooms when they've been able to redecorate or rearrange the room in a new and inviting way.

- Get your child into some good pre-sleep routines. Where possible, keep your child to a regular bed time, even over weekends and holidays.

- A warm bath and a milky drink can help your child to wind down towards a night of sleep. Whilst it's wonderful to spend time reading to our younger children, try to ensure that you say goodnight *before* your child actually goes to sleep. Your child needs to know that she can fall asleep on her own.

- Anxious children sometimes like to have a light-hearted book, comic or magazine next to their beds so that, if they wake up, they can use the material to settle down again without getting out of their beds.

- If your child does come to look for you in the night (this often happens), lead him back into his room, help him to settle, if he uses music, switch it on, and then return to your room. Don't wait until he falls asleep! It's hard, but if you do this, you will probably end up back at square one.

- I've found that it's easier to tackle sleep difficulties on the back of another worry-related success. If your child has overcome worry in another part of her life, then she already has some understanding of the principles involved (e.g. containing the worry, relaxation and right thinking). So you might want to pick an easier 'training area' before you ask your child to change her anxiety-based sleep habits.

- I remind older and more insightful children that sleep is something that happens to us; we can't force it. In fact, the more we try to go to sleep, the harder it gets. So we talk about habits that 'allow' sleep to happen to us. For me, this starts with relaxing the muscles around the eyes. As we fall asleep, our eyes aren't looking at anything specific whereas when we're tense or anxious we tend to keep our eyes very focused. As they allow their eyes to close, many children benefit from using some variation of progressive muscle relaxation. For instance, a child might like to imagine that a warm, honey-like substance is flowing into their bodies from the toes up and that, as it passes over each part of the body, the muscles become more and more deeply relaxed.

- Do notice your child's efforts, and let her know how proud you are of any progress that she makes.

- *Sleep-outs:*
  - One of the most common obstacles to progress with sleep-outs is that they don't happen often enough. Remember, practice is vital when it comes to learning new emotional habits. So if your child wants to get more confident in this area, she really needs to sleep out fairly regularly.

  - Perhaps you and your child can think of a relative or family friend, who wouldn't mind being used as a practice site. As your child spends the next four Friday evenings at Granny's house, she can practise some of the self-soothing and calming exercises listed above. Once she has acclimatised to this, she might then be ready to practise her abilities with a trusted friend.

  - Many sensitive children find that it's best to practice 'sleep outs' during the holidays. Because they're under less pressure and stress, children are often more socially adventurous during long holidays, and it's also reassuring to know that they have plenty of recovery time if things don't go all that smoothly.

  - Remember, many sensitive children prefer and need some quiet private time at the end of a busy week. So don't give your child the idea that she has to *like* sleep-outs. We just want her to know that she *can* do it.

References:

Adler, H. (1994). *N. L. P. the new art and science of getting what you want.* Pitakus Books: London.

Aron, E.N. (2002) The Highly Sensitive Child: Helping Our Children Thrive When The World Overwhelms Them. Broadway Books: New York

Buber, M. (1937). *I and Thou,* trans. Walter Kaufmann (1990) New York: Simon & Schuster.

Buckingham, M. & Clifton, D. O. (2001). *Now, Discover Your Strengths.* New York: The Free Press.

Carr, S. (2002). *Love and Fear in Executive Coaching.* Fitzgerald, C. & Garvey Berger, J. (Eds.) California: Davies-Black Publishing.

Caspi, A., harrington, H., Milne, B., Amell, J.W., Theodore, R.F., & Moffitt, T.E. (2003). Children's behavioural styles at age 3 are linked to their adult personality traits at age 26. *Journal of Personality, 71,* 495-514.

Corbis, B.C. (2004). *What Makes Teens Tick.* Time, May 10, 2004, p.59.

Covey, S. R. (2004). *The 8th Habit: From Effectiveness to Greatness.* New York: Simon & Schuster.

Csikszentmihalyi, M. & Csikszentmihalyi, I. S.(1988). *Optimal Experience, psychological studies of flow in consciousness.* Cambridge: Cambridge University Press.

Damon, W. (2005). *Noble Purpose.* Templeton Foundation Press.

De Botton, A. (2004). *Status Anxiety.* London: Penguin.

Deci, E. L. (1971). *Effects of externally-mediated rewards on intrinsic motivation.* Journal of Personality and Social Psychology, 18, pp.105-115.

Dienstbier, R. A. & Pytlik Zillig, L. M. (2002). *Toughness.* In *Handbook of Positive Psychology.* New York: Oxford University Press.

Doctorow, E. L. (1982). *The Book of Daniel.* London: Pan Books.

DuPont Spencer, E., DuPont, R. & DuPont, C. M. (2003). *The Anxiety Cure for Children: A Guide for Parents.* New Jersey: Wiley.

Eisenberger, R. Kuhlman, D. M., & Cotterell, N. (1992). *Effects of social values, effort training, and goal structure on task persistence.* Journal of Research in Personality, 26, p.258-272.

Emmons, R. A. & Crumpler, C. A. (2000). *Gratitude as Human Strength: appraising the evidence.* Journal of Social and Clinical Psychology, 19, 56-59

Emmons, R. A. & Shelton, C. M. *Gratitude and the science of positive psychology.* In Snyder, C.R. & Lopez, S. J. (Eds.) (2002) *Handbook of Positive Psychology.* Oxford University Press: Oxford.

Fishman, D. B. (1999). *The Case for Pragmatic Psychology,* New York: New York University Press.

Fromm, E. (1956). *The Art of Loving.* New York: Harper and Row.

Gallup survey results on gratitude, adults and teenagers. *Emerging trends, 20, 9.*

Gilligan, S. (1997). *The Courage to Love. Principles and practices of Self-Relations psychotherapy.* W.W. Norton & Company: New York London.

Glasser, H. N. & Easley, J. L. (2003). *Transforming the Difficult Child. The Nurtured Heart Approach.* Nashville: Vaughan Printing.

Gleason, J. B. & Weintraub, S. (1976). *The acquisitions of routine in child language.* Language in Society, 5, 129-136.

Goleman, D. (1998). *Working with Emotional Intelligence.* London: Bloomsbury Publishers.

Goleman, D. (1995). *Emotional Intelligence,* London: Bloomsbury Publishers.

Gottman, J. (1994). *Why marriages succeed or fail and how you can make yours last.* New York: Simon & Schuster.

Gottman, J. M. & Declaire, J. (1997). *Raising an Emotionally Intelligent Child. The Heart of Parenting.* New York: Fireside.

Gottman, J. M. & Silver, N. (2000). *The Seven Principles for Making Marriage Work. A Practical Guide from the Country's Foremost Relationship Expert.*

Habermas, J. (1993). *Justification and Application: remarks on discourse ethics,* translated by Cirian Cronin. Cambridge, UK: Polity Press.

Hart, A. D. (1992). *Stress and your child: The hidden reason why your child may be moody, resentful, or insecure.* U.S.A. W Publishing Group.

Harre, R. & Van Langenhove, L. (1991). *Varieties of positioning.* Journal for the Theory of Social Behaviour, 21, p.393-407.

Hermans, H. J. M. & Kempen, H. J. G. (1993). *The dialogical self: Meaning as movement.* San Diego: Academic Press.

Hobart Mowrer, O. (1964). *The new Group Therapy.* Mass Market Paperback.

Hoyt, M. F. (1996) (Ed.) *Constructive Therapies Vol. 2.* New York: Guilford Press.

Hunter, J. P. & Csikszentmihalyi, M. (2003). *The Positive Psychology of Interested Adolescents.* Journal of Youth and Adolescence, Vol. 32, No. 1, February, p.27-35.

Jackson, S.A. & Csikszentmihalyi, M. (1999) *Flow in Sports: The Keys to Optimal Experiences and Performances.* Champaign: Human Kinetics

Kagan, J. & Snidman, N. (2004). *The Long Shadow of Temperament.* Cambridge, Mass.: Harvard University Press.

Kagan, J. (1998). *How We Become Who We Are.* Family Therapy Network Symposium.

Katzenbach, J R. (2000). *Peak Performance,* Boston. Harvard Business School Press.

Klein, M. (1957) *Envy and Gratitude. A Study of Unconscious Sources.* New York: Basic Books

Larson, R. & Richards, M. (1991). *Boredom in the middle school years: Blaming schools versus blaming students.* American Journal of Education 99, p.418-443.

Larson, R. W. (2000). *Toward a Psychology of Positive Youth Development.* American Psychologist, Vol. 55, No. 1, p.170-183.

Lerner, H. G. (1993). *The Dance of Deception. Pretending and truth-telling in women's lives.* Harpercollins

Leunig, M. (1990). *A Common Prayer.* North Blackburn, Victoria, Australia: Collins Dove.

Loehr, J. E. & Schwartz, T. (2005). *The Power of Full Engagement.* The Free Press: New York

Miller, W .R. & Rollnick, S. (2002). *Motivational Interviewing.* New York: The Guilford Press.

Morris, T. L. & March, J. S. (Eds.) (2004). *Anxiety Disorders in Children and Adolescents*. (2nd Ed.). New York: The Guilford Press.

Olweus, D. (1993). *Bullying at School*. Oxford: Blackwell.

Overwalle, F. V., Mervielde, I. & De Schuyter, J. (1995). *Structural modelling of the relationships between attributional dimensions, emotions and performance of college freshmen*. Cognition and emotion, 9, 59-85.

Payne, M. (2000). *Narrative Therapy, an Introduction for Counsellors*. London: Sage.

Peterson, C. & Seligman, M.E.P (2004). *Character Strengths and Virtues. A Handbook and Classification*. New York: Oxford University Press New York.

Rapee, R. M., Wignall, A., Hudson, J. L. & Schneiring, C. A. (2000). *Treating Anxious Children and Adolescents. An Evidence-Based Approach*. Canada: New Harbinger Press.

Rath, T. (2007). *Strengths Finder 2.0*. New York, NY Gallup Press

Real, T. (2002). *Awful Truth*. Psychotherapy Networker, November/ December.

Roberts, L. M., Spreitzer, G., Dutton, J., Quinn, R., Heaphy, E. & Barker, B. *How to Play to Your Strengths. Harvard Business Review*. January, 2005.

Rosenbaum, R. & Dyckman, J. (1996) *No Self? No Problem! Actualizing Empty Self in Psychotherapy*. In *Constructive Therapies Vol. 2*. pp.238-274. (Hoyt, M. Ed).

Rossouw, D. (2002). *Business Ethics in Africa*. Cape Town: Oxford University Press Southern Africa.

Schulman, M. (2002) *How We Become Moral. The Sources of Moral Motivation. In Handbook of Positive Psychology*, Snyder, C. R. & Lopez, S. J. (Eds.) New York: Oxford University Press.

Schwartz, C. et al. *Inhibited and Uninhibited Infants 'Grown Up': Adult Amygdala response to Novel Versus newly Familiar Faces*, Science 399 (2003) p.1952-1953.

Seigel, D. J. (1999). *The Developing Mind: How Relationships and the Brain Interact to Shape Who We Are*. New York: Guilford Press.

Siegel, D. J. & Hartzell, M. (2004). *Parenting from the Inside Out: How a deeper self-understanding can help you raise children who thrive*. Penguin: New York

Seligman, M. (2002). *Authentic Happiness*. New York: The Free Press: New York.

Shatte, A.J., Gillham, J.E., & Reivich, K. *Promoting Hope in Children and Adolescents.* in *The Science of Optimism and Hope. Research Essays in Honour of Martin E.P. Seligman (Gillham, J.E. Ed).* London: Templeton Foundation Press.

Simon, R. (1999). *Don't just do something, Sit there.* Family Therapy Networker, January/ February.

Smedes, L.B (1996) The Art of Forgiving: When You Need to Forgive and Don't Know How. Nashville, TN: Moorings

Soloveychik, S. (2006). *Parenting for everyone.*

Sroufe, L. A., & Fleeson, J. (1988). *Relationships within families: Mutual influences.* In R. Hinde & J. Stevenson-Hinde (Eds.), *The coherence of family relations* (pp. 27-47). Oxford, UK: Oxford University Press.

Starnes, D. M. & Zinser, O. (1983). *The effect of problem difficulty, locus of control, and sex on task persistence.* Journal of General Psychology, 108. p.249-255.

Stern, D. (2004). *The Present Moment in Psychotherapy and Everyday Life.* New York: W. W. Norton.

Sykes Wylie, M. & Simon, R. (2002) *Discoveries from the Black Box.* Psychotherapy Networker, September/ October.

Taffel, R. & Blau, M. (1999). *Nurturing Good Children Now.* New York: Golden Books New York.

Tan, P. C. (1974). *The interpretation of prophecy.*

Thomas, A., Chess, S., & Birch, H. G. (1968). *Temperament and behaviour disorders in children.* New York: New York University Press.

Watson, D. (2000). *Mood and temperament.* New York: Guilford.

Wehrenberg, M. *Anxiety Management Techniques. Psychotherapy Networker* (September/October 2005).

Walker, L. J. & Pitts, R. C. (1998). *Naturalistic conceptions of moral maturity.* Developmental Psychology, 34, 403-419.

White, M. & Epston, D. (1990) *Narrative Means to Therapeutic Ends.* New York: Norton.

Yancy, P. (2001). *Soul Survivor.* London: Hodder & Stoughton.

6193215R0

Made in the USA
Lexington, KY
15 August 2010